ORDINARY WOMAN
EXTRAORDINARY GOD

JILL LISA BILLS

Write to Jill at:
OWExtraordinaryGod@gmail.com

DEDICATION

This book is for all the GOOD NEWSERS. I pray you're encouraged to stay the course; inviting others to "come and see" our Lord and Savior Jesus Christ and to believe on no other name on earth or in heaven.

To Patrick, my beloved, thank you for being my BFF and supporting me while creating this book.

PROLOGUE

I call myself ordinary for many reasons. First, I haven't received any awards for outstanding achievement like Teacher of the Year, I haven't had a cause that I created a nonprofit for, I haven't made a ton of money, I haven't been bit by a shark, and I haven't played a professional sport.

I'm probably a lot like you. I have worked hard and tried to be a person of good character.

I spent 27 years in public schools teaching pre-k through third grade and elementary school counseling. After leaving the public-school system, I spent three years as a child and teen therapist at a large behavioral health clinic.

Second, I'm also ordinary to look at. I am on the short side with crazy curly hair. I like being active with biking, hiking, kayaking, and group fitness classes, but I lack the great hand eye coordination for competitive sports.

The third reason I think I am ordinary is I was raised in the mid-west in a middle-class family. My family experienced some of the typical ups and downs that other families experience, but no tragic accidents or illnesses until my Dad got sick. You'll hear more about that later.

But I am not ordinary in God's eyes and heart. His word, the Bible, says that we each are *fearfully and wonderfully made, knitted together in our mother's womb. (Psalm 139:13-14)*

I write this book as a woman who knows The Extraordinary God, the maker of heaven and earth. I see myself as a messenger with an important message I would like you to hear. I hope and pray that you will take this message to heart and have a personal encounter with The Extraordinary God, the triune of God the Father, His Son Jesus, and The Holy Spirit.

Notes: To help with the readability and flow of this text, all scripture from God's inerrant Word, the Bible, have been bolded and italicized. The scripture location (book, chapter, and verse) have been added so you can easily look them up for yourself in the Bible. All scripture has been taken from the New International Version (NIV) Bible.

TABLE OF CONTENTS

INTRODUCTION: EMBRACING A NEW SEASON

I was just winding down the last week of a twelve-week period of preparing for my launch into retirement or "refirement." My husband, Patrick, was in Florida supervising the renovation of our villa, (Florida lingo for an attached condo), while I remained in Michigan. Patrick and I both knew that he was much more equipped to deal with a construction project than I was. I get too anxious with remodeling, there's too much waiting around, and too many decisions to be made.

My time in Michigan was devoted to finishing strong at my place of employment, a large behavioral health clinic where I counseled kids, teens, and their families. I used this time also for inner spiritual growth. Since this was the first and only time in my life that I lived alone and with no television, I wanted to spend my extra time connecting with

Jesus. What an awesome experience this was! One of the revelations was how God's story written in the Bible intertwines with my life.

Part of a message given by a missionary at a Mother's Day Tea during those 12 weeks was that at various times of our lives we feel connected to a person from the Bible or a situation in the Bible. The speaker's example in her life was feeling like the boy with the 2 fish and 3 loaves of bread during Jesus' Sermon on the Mount. The boy was inexperienced and had little to offer but was willing to give all he had to Jesus. Since this was the missionary's first encounter with going overseas to minister to a different culture, this is how she felt.

The encouraging part was how Jesus took those few items and blessed them and multiplied them to feed 5000 hungry people. This then encouraged the speaker to move forward and trust that her meager offerings would be blessed and the spiritually hungry people she was going to serve would be satisfied with the word of God. I could relate to this teaching because I too, am ordinary without any super spectacular skills. However, what I do have is a vibrant relationship with Jesus, who is super spectacular in every imaginable way.

During these twelve weeks, questions and comments would surface in conversation with just about everyone I knew. "What are you going to do in Florida? You are going to work, right? You know you're too young to retire." This badgering really put me in a state of confusion because, for the first time in my life, I was seeking God first to order my steps. I would vacillate between patiently waiting on God's timing to being Squirrel Girl (my nickname for myself when my mind would jump from possibility to possibility).

Like a squirrel, I decided to store up all the possibilities of work or volunteering I could do in Florida. I created a list of twenty or so worthwhile, God honoring activities that fit my skill set: I could get certified in Florida and counsel people, work on a rapid response team for emergencies, do marriage counseling, hold babies and play with toddlers when single moms are working, be a coffee barista at church, serve as a reading tutor, write children's books (I actually started writing a children's book during this time alone), take Bible classes and art classes, do human traffic/trauma counseling and the list went on and on.

I thank God for the other Jesus girls in my life. Finally, a friend and co-worker suggested I pack, move, unpack, and settle in before I make any big decisions or commitments. Then, while visiting Patrick during the renovation, the pastor at church said during a sermon, "A spirit of confusion is not from God." I thank God for this pastor who speaks the truth of God. These two messages gave me peace about waiting on God's perfect timing...at least most of the time.

Back to the last week of this time of preparation. I had taught my last women's Sunday school Bible class, I felt like I was ready to move, and I had said my last good byes to my Peeps (the kids and teens I counseled), friends, and family. Then, a word from the Holy Spirit, "Before you write books for children I want you to write a book about your life with ME, titled 'Ordinary Woman Extraordinary God'." I pondered that for a while. "Ok," I questioned it, "Me?"

"What do I have to write about? Who would want to read about an ordinary woman? Don't people like to read about the rich and famous?" Much later the true focus of the book appeared; sharing the events in my life leading up to my repentance and finally recognizing The Sovereign Holy

God and how he became the personal God of my daily life through the believe in God the Son Jesus.

Wanting to be obedient, I started writing some ideas in a journal, but then would stop and doubt that *"God, the Almighty maker of heaven and earth" (Psalm 146:6)* had given me this assignment to write this book. Then I received confirmation. I had just come home from a small group meeting with women who wanted to learn how to knit. Writing this book had been on my mind. I checked my phone for messages and a friend from my Michigan church had texted this:

"Guess what?!!??"

I responded with "what?" and she asked if we could talk. And did we talk!

My friend calls herself "The Chicken Lady" because she raises chickens and sells the eggs. She told me her amazing story about getting her book published. I didn't even know she was writing a book. She had made inquiries on a publishing website. This site contacted her and offered her a contract to publish. As she was telling her story, I was thinking, why did she call me with this news?" When I asked her this question she said, "Because I felt like I needed to." I felt like this was a reminder from God, it was time to get this book written! So here it is! A testimony to how God is sovereign <u>and</u> close <u>and</u> personal to the people who choose to follow Him.

I will praise you, O LORD, with all my heart;
I will tell of all your wonders.
I will be glad and rejoice in you;
I will sing praise to your name, O Most High
Psalm 9:1-2

BC: BEFORE CHRIST

CHILDHOOD AND YOUTH

Where to begin? How about right at the beginning? I was born in the spring of 1963, the third daughter to my parents Norbert and Rita. According to my mother's notes in my baby book, I was born small at 5 pounds, 6 ounces and 19 inches long. I progressed well, probably because each entry mentioned that I was a good eater, liked to eat, or tried new foods.

I was the baby of the family for four and half years. I liked that position and was quite content. Then my youngest sister Jackie joined our family of all girls- Jenifer, Janet, Jill, and Jackie. I'm told I didn't do well getting booted out of the baby of the family position. Alright, let's face it, I was jealous. I didn't like all the attention Jackie was receiving, but I wasn't very smart about it either. I would pinch her and wake her up thinking this would show her who was boss! Then one of my parents would pick her up to soothe her and this just made me more jealous. Oh the silly thinking of a four-year-old.

My childhood was mostly happy. We went to church together as a family on Sundays to St. Bedes Catholic

Church. My sisters and I also attended catechism, Catholic religious education, one afternoon a week at church once we entered first grade. We didn't pray before meals, at bedtime, or at any time that I can recall. Knowing now that God is omnipresent, He was there even though as a child I wasn't particularly aware of His presence.

We had many family get-togethers, sometimes at our house and sometimes at aunts and uncles or grandparents. My dad especially liked getting the family together. He hosted holiday parties, pig roasts, birthdays, first communions, and informal drop-ins. I remember my dad calling his brother, my Uncle Tony and asking him if he wanted some company. That was my dad's way of inviting our family over.

These parties always included lots of food, Polish food at Christmas, mom's yummy macaroni and potato salad for summer parties, and of course roasted pork at the pig roasts. These parties also included alcohol like beer and mixed drinks. Soooo… sometimes it got rowdy and loud.

I was known to have had enough of the parties and would get myself ready for bed and go to sleep. My mom told me of the time she was checking up on the kids at a party at our house and couldn't find me. None of my sisters or cousins knew where I was. Finally, my mom found me in my bed sleeping, with teeth brushed and pajamas on, all at the age of four.

My parents took my sisters and I on many family vacations. We explored our home state of Michigan during these vacations. I remember seeing the Taquemanon Falls in the upper peninsula for the first time and thinking it looked like root beer with the foam. Riding rental bikes around Mackinaw Island was quite an adventure and a day trip to

Huron City provided an education of the early pioneers of the Michigan thumb.

My family also took yearly winter trips to Florida. I loved the feel of the warm moist air on our faces as we exited the plane on the runway in Florida. We either stayed in Clearwater or the Fort Wilderness Camp Ground at Disney World. I have many good memories of swimming at the Holiday Inn in Clearwater. My oldest sister Jenifer told me of a time when I was four years old and wasn't looking where I was going, and I fell in the deep end of the pool and she had to rescue me.

We played miniature golf next door to the hotel and the best part was when the tiger on the last hole talked. At the time, I didn't see the owner speaking on the intercom pretending to be the tiger. The funniest Florida memory was the year we drove from Michigan with a pop-up camper. We arrived at the Disney World campground in the dark. My dad was unfamiliar with setting up the camper so that took a long time. Then with no TV, my dad did the voices of a sitcom popular at the time. We laughed and laughed. I really liked being together as a family. It made me feel safe and secure.

When I was in the fourth grade my nervous temperament escalated to extremely anxious. I had really enjoyed school and I even played school in a classroom I made under the basement stairs at our house. Now, I was worried that I would get into trouble at school. I thought the teacher might think I was a trouble maker. Almost everything in my life created worry and anxiety. Well, the way I thought about everything created distress. I was a quiet rule follower.

On Monday mornings, I would start vomiting from having a nervous tummy which sometimes resulted in staying home from school. Then my anxiety would increase on Tuesday morning and the cycle went on and on. This lasted most of the school year. Looking back, it would have been beneficial for me to have seen a counselor. Instead, my mom provided extra time for me and was encouraging. My dad got frustrated with my behavior. My nickname became "Quiver Chin" because before I started to cry my chin would shake.

When I was ten years old we moved from the suburbs of Detroit to my dad's childhood farm in the thumb of Michigan. This move was a culture shock for the whole family. It was too dark at night, too quiet, and there was no shopping nearby. The worst was getting snowed in during the winter. What I did like was the small country elementary school. My favorite subject was reading. I made new friends and loved that my mom was a volunteer recess lady. My anxiety was lessening due to the slower paced lifestyle.

Then middle school and boys! Do I need to say more? I tried out and made the 7th and 8th grade cheerleading squad. Quite a feat since I am clapping impaired and can't keep a beat.

One of the other cheerleaders and I became close friends and she invited me to her Wednesday night youth group at her Methodist church. When I asked for parental permission my mom said, "absolutely not, we are Catholic." I heard that statement many times growing up and I never knew what it meant. I would just repeat it back to whoever asked me to do something that I wasn't allowed to do.

True confession time: one time I snuck out and went to the Wednesday youth group. It was so much fun. I could hardly believe it was considered a church activity. We played balloon volleyball, had snacks, and had what I would consider a Jesus character-building teaching. There was also conversation about what was taught and lots of laughing. I would have loved to have gone back, but it would have meant lying to my parents again. So, I didn't. *(Honor thy father and mother. Exodus 20:12)* But I never forgot the wonderful experience.

In my opinion, our country home was party central. I tried alcohol for the first time in middle school. I didn't like the taste of it, but I thought it made me cool. Many other kids my age were experimenting with drinking, too. The young men working for my family's egg production business, located close to our home, often stopped by our home and drank alcohol. As I reflect back on this time of drinking, smoking, as well as unsupervised teenagers and young adult males and females, this was not a particularly good combination, as you can imagine!

My dad got restless being out in the country. In my first year of high school we moved from the thumb of Michigan to a town further south. The town was bigger with more amenities. That move was hard in many ways. I felt like an ugly duckling with my kinky-curly hair. Back then in the late 1970's early 1980's there weren't any good curly hair products like there are today. My insecurity worsened when the upperclassmen at the new high school called out derogatory names at me while I walked past the heating registers that they sat on like thrones. I would definitely not want to relive my high school years. At that time, my family was still attending the once a week obligation mass at the Catholic church.

I had a high school best friend. We both lived in town, so we had fun using our babysitting money to visit fast food places and the local drugstore. We also attended parties on the weekends and drank alcohol. I usually threw up and had hangovers, but I still thought it was cool. The alcohol made me feel relaxed and resulted in some very risky and irresponsible behavior. In spite, of this rebellious behavior, I was a good student and earned decent grades. I was invited to join the honor society and even graduated 10th in my high school senior class.

My dad became extremely ill shortly after we had moved. He had many health conditions: diabetes, arthritis, heart failure, weight loss, edema, and low energy. My dad being sick created stress and changed my family dramatically. Since my dad was self-employed in a heating and air conditioning business and working sporadically in a poor economy, the money was tight. My mom told my sisters and I that if we wanted clothes, make-up, cars, and spending money then we would have to work. I feel this helped me to develop a strong work ethic <u>and</u> financial insecurities. The days of big family parties were over and replaced with a gloom over the family. My dad was a proud man who generously helped others, however he couldn't ask for help or accept help. He kept the knowledge of his illness private. Even his own siblings didn't know the extent of his condition.

Back to the high school days. Since this was not my favorite season of life, I tried to pin point why it was unpleasant. In my opinion, the teen years are a time of searching and unrest, comparing and competition, and a time when parents really need to be involved in their teen's lives. High school is like a giant social experiment where many adolescents enter and try to exit more mature, more intelligent, and with the least number of emotional wounds and scars as possible.

I did get smarter, I matured some, but sustained some emotional wounds. I was anxious most days, not about academics, but about the people. Like I mentioned, I felt less in the looks department and high school was mostly about the outer beauty not the inner beauty. I distinctly remember a sad time during a class called Radio and TV. The teacher had passed out slips of paper which had the name of a classmate on it. Our assignment was to take turns and orally describe the person on the slip of paper without using their name. The other students would guess who was being described. A male student started out by saying something like,

"This girl is wearing white painter's pants, is kind of chunky, has ugly frizzy hair, and her face is covered with pimples."

When I heard how he described me, I put my head down on the desk and quietly sobbed. I felt so alone and ugly. What I didn't know then but know now is that when people get critical of others it's a way of elevating their own self-worth by squashing someone else. Boy, was I squashed. I don't recall anyone, even the teacher, reaching out to me. The other students were grateful that they weren't the one getting humiliated. In today's world all the name calling would be considered bullying.

I was reminded of this incident a few years ago when I counseled teens who were anxious and struggling with high school. I would intentionally confirm, affirm, encourage, compliment, and help the teens find their best qualities and know that I believed in them. Sometimes just one caring adult can make a huge positive difference in the life of a teen.

I think of Romans 8:28 in the Bible, *"and we know that in all things God works for the good of those who love Him, who have been called according to HIS purpose."* God used this negative experience and other experiences in my teen years to help me empathize with the teens I counseled later in my life. God was so awesome at changing the way I looked at my past negative experiences and made them useful in building Godly character in me and in others.

Another verse comes to my mind and it's from *2 Corinthians 1:3-4 "Praise be to the God and Father of our Lord Jesus Christ, the Father of compassion and the God of all comfort, who comforts us in all our troubles, so that we can comfort those in any trouble with the comfort we ourselves have received from God."* I now look at troubles very differently in my life than I did before trusting and receiving Jesus as my Lord and Savior. Instead of seeing troubles and problems negatively, now I view problems as a part of life and God's way of maturing me, ridding me of ungodly character traits, and giving me the ability to help others by comforting, strengthening, and encouraging them, which results in hope.

By the end of high school my dad had become increasingly sick and had to go on disability. My mom was stressed and preoccupied with his doctor's appointments and not knowing exactly what was wrong or how to help my dad. I remember vividly the time I suggested it could be cancer. My mom about bit my head off and said something like, "How could you even think that, let alone say it?" Back then in the late 1970's and early 1980's, cancer was most likely deadly and no one wanted to acknowledge the C word. I don't recall any family prayers for my dad's health condition and the well-being of our family at the time. There was just worry and the stuffing of questions and feelings.

I affectionately call my family of origin "stuffers." If we were not getting along with each other, instead of talking to the sister that we were having the problem with, we would instead talk behind their back to a different sister. Consequently, there are many old wounds and unaddressed issues that are like lumps underneath the carpet that to this day we still trip over and unfortunately, have superficial relationships with each other.

Even though I didn't feel close to God at this time of my life, I know God was there protecting me from the profound consequences that could have happened from the foolish decisions and behavior I had during my teen years. *"For God will command his angels concerning you to guard you in all your ways." Psalm 91:11* Most of my friends and I would drive our parents' cars after we had been drinking. It was a miracle that none of us were in an accident or the cause of an accident. I'm thankful my mom could see through some of our crazy plans as really drinking excursions and say no to them.

Not something I condone nor want to glorify was my experimenting with drugs during high school. In my neighborhood, three teens had become drug dealers and were easy access to substances like pot, speed, and acid. In order to fit in and be cool, I tried each one of the mentioned drugs once. Thank God, I had such negative reactions I never tried them again. The pot made me so out of it and slow. I was driving 15 mph in a 35-mph zone. I was also allergic to pot and my eyes started swelling shut. The speed made my heart race so fast that as I laid in bed I thought I was going to die of a heart attack. Lastly, the acid gave me hallucinations and I took off running in a cornfield at an outdoor party. These actions could have had serious negative consequences, but with God's protection I was spared.

Since I'm sharing all the junk and sin from my before Christ years I can't leave out promiscuity. Most of my teenage peers who I socialized with were sexually active. Our 1981 class saying was "party, sex, and fun we are the class of 1981". I cringe just writing that down. To fit in or fulfill a need for love (or both), I became sexually active with my first boyfriend during my senior year of high school. It was irresponsible and not what God wants for the unmarried. As I reflect on my college years I feel connected to Gomer in the Bible. Her story is told in the book of Hosea. Gomer was also a promiscuous young woman looking for love in all the wrong places. *"Oh Lord, remember not the sins of my youth and my rebellious ways: according to Your love remember me." Psalm 25:7*

THE GAP

After graduation from high school I had a gap year where I worked fulltime as a receptionist at a hair salon. I really enjoyed the work and learned a great deal about hair and skin care. I worked and went out with a new boyfriend and his wild friends. My dad's health continued to deteriorate with many hospital stays. I found it difficult to visit him or anyone else in the hospital. I'm a little better now, knowing how much the hospital patient appreciates the visit. I think of the words of Jesus, *"...I was sick, and you looked after me..." Matthew 25:36.* This scripture helps me visiting the sick in the hospital now.

I didn't receive very much guidance for college or career planning from my high school counselor or my family before graduation. My bosses at the hair salon encouraged me to apply to college. I remember one of them saying to me, "You know we don't expect you to stay here for a career. You should think about college." I decided to apply to Michigan State University. I remember being so excited when I got my acceptance letter which opened with the greeting, "Congratulations You Are a Spartan!" When I showed the letter to my mother, I didn't get the same excitement. She responded with, "And how are you going to pay for that?"

Well, I hadn't gotten that far in my planning, so I said, "I don't know?"

My mom made an appointment with the high school guidance counselor and both her and I went to the appointment. Mind you, I already had graduated. I was the first in my family to attend college, so the information received at this appointment was valuable. Financial aid paperwork was filled out by my mom and due to my father's health condition, good grades, and my high ACT score I qualified for help. The financial help and savings from my earnings at the hair salon were not enough to meet the financial demands for college and living expenses so I worked a part-time job or two throughout my college years right up to graduation.

These many part-time jobs during college, prior to my career position as a teacher were: babysitting, fast food restaurants, family businesses, bookstore warehouse, women's clothing stores, receptionist, office aide, and other retail stores to name a few. Some of the jobs I worked at the same time. I had the youthful energy to burn the candle at both ends.

I was off to college in the fall of 1982. It was shocking in many ways: being away from home for the first time, so many different cultures, and unfortunately some more poor decisions. I went to the bar with friends and roommates and we also went to parties. The alcohol made me feel fun and carefree. I did manage to earn a respectable grade point average that first semester. *"...Please my Lord do not hold against us the sin we have so foolishly committed." Numbers 12:11*

My dad's health continued to decline that fall and my second oldest sister Janet and her fiancé, joined the family heating and air conditioning company full-time. When I came home for Christmas break it was clear to me my dad was nearing the end of his life. He had lost so much weight, slept most of the time, and was in a great deal of pain. He was rushed to the hospital a few days after Christmas and passed away on December 28, 1982.

Upon an autopsy, requested by mom, it was determined that my father had an old large scar on his heart pointing to a heart attack a long time ago and that he had cardiomyopathy. Cardiomyopathy is a disease of the heart muscles. The muscles become enlarged, thick, or rigid, which weaken the heart and the heart is less able to pump blood through the body and keep regular heartbeats. My family finally received the answer to my father's declining health condition which resulted in his death.

Due to the conditions of my financial aid, I had to return to college for the winter trimester. This was an exceedingly tough time in my life. I didn't attend any grief counseling and I didn't think to seek counseling through the university or the church. The two college roommates I roomed with at that time, were also best friends. They were involved in their own lives and we were all young, so they were not any help during this time. I started going home every weekend to be with my mom and sisters. We all muddled through the grief reactions of anger, sadness, shock, and finally acceptance. My mom, however, talked about my dad as if he were still living right up until she received the diagnosis of dementia in 2010.

The Catholic Church has some man-made beliefs about death. It is a Catholic belief that a deceased member is in a place called purgatory waiting to find out if he or she has made it to heaven. Family and friends of the deceased can pay for a church service (mass) in honor of the dead person and to pray their way out of purgatory and into heaven. At that time and now that does not make sense to me and cannot be found in the Bible. The Bible states, *"For God so loved the world that he gave his one and only Son, that whoever believes in him shall not perish but have eternal life."* John 3:16. Jesus Christ, the Son of God, died on the cross to pay the price of our sins, and accepting this free gift allows a person eternal life with him. The individual choice of believing in Jesus Christ is made when a person is living. A choice I have made, and I hope you do too because no one can be prayed up to heaven, after they have died. It is a choice as long as we are alive and yet breathing.

I muddled my way through the next 4 years of college. Since I had to work 2 jobs and attend school full-time, I was unable to put in the necessary hours of study to earn great grades. My grades were average, and I had a challenging time deciding on a major. Two of my college jobs were political/government; a page (errand person) for the state house of representatives and an election year worker for the State Republican Party. These jobs were interesting and led me to a major in Political Science. An interesting major, but it didn't lend itself to too many career opportunities.

I remember trying to attend the Catholic church twice while in college. The first time was shorty after my father had passed. I was looking for comfort and hope but didn't get it and left the mass just as empty as I had when I entered the church. The second time I went to the student Catholic

Church on campus. This time I saw other college coeds who looked just as confused as I was. Most were attending because of a sense of guilt and obligation from their childhoods.

I was so happy to finally graduate from college and start earning a "real" income. Reality set in quickly, when my search for a political science job produced one offer. The offer was to be the finance person for a candidate running for governor in the state of Minnesota. I had gone to Washington, DC after graduation to attend a three-day training on campaign finance. A connection at the conference was how I ended up in Minnesota.

Fortunately, a college friend had moved to a suburb of Minneapolis for a job and I was able to room with her. It is comical to look back at this short-lived job. I was so not qualified to step in and oversee raising money for a candidate I didn't even know and outside of my home state. I think I lasted six weeks before the campaign manager released me from my duties. I drove back to Michigan with no job, no job prospects, and no money.

I moved back home with my mother and younger sister Jackie and worked a retail job to make ends meet. I remember going to the Catholic Church my family attended in distress about my lack of career opportunities. It was early afternoon and only one other person was in the church. I had no experience praying and made a petition prayer for a career job to my dead father! If only I had known to pray to God our heavenly Father, in the name of Jesus Christ. My dad didn't help me get a political/government job, but God was working out a better plan, for me and for my life.

God's plan incorporated my childhood dream of being an elementary school teacher. As I noted earlier, I loved going to school and starting in first grade I began to play "school" in the space under the basement stairs. When my first-grade teacher put extra worksheets and construction paper in the scrap box I would quickly confiscate them, take them home, and use them for teaching in my classroom. Sometimes my sisters would be my students, sometimes neighborhood kids, and sometimes dolls and stuffed animals. It was such great fun.

My mother had found a "help wanted" listing for substitute teachers in our local newspaper and encouraged me to apply, reminding me of my earlier desires of being a teacher. So, in the fall of 1986, I started substitute teaching. It was decent money and I was called between 5:00-5:30am most every school day to fill in for a teacher. I would substitute teach in elementary, middle school, and high school. At the same time, I also applied to attend college at the University of Michigan-Flint. I found out I could take teacher methodology classes, complete a student teaching internship, and earn elementary teacher credentials. God was steering me towards a career that fit my personality and love of children a far better career than any job in the political science field could have ever been.

The next year was a whirlwind of activity and life changes! Along with substitute teaching nearly every school day, attending college courses in the afternoons and evenings, I added a second job at the local drug store on the weekends. I barely had time to eat a meal at home. On days that I was substitute teaching and went to class, I fell back to munching on my favorite snack of goldfish crackers. One particular day, I was sneakily eating them in the library while collecting information for a research paper. Back in 1987 research was conducted by using microfiche, not the internet. I can vaguely remember the complete process of microfiche, but what I do remember was the vast amounts of time it took to find a scholarly article and make a copy of it. I was in the initial stages of this research, eating my goldfish crackers when I hear someone behind me saying, "There's no eating cookies in the library."

I was quick to answer back, "They are not cookies they are crackers."

I thought I was in trouble by the library police, but when I turned around and found the person who was talking to me, I saw a handsome man. I had seen him before, working out at the recreation building. I thought he was cute even at that time. Oh, and he wasn't the library police, but was flirting with me.

After a short conversation, we found out that we had the same class and professor, same research paper assignment, but attended two different sections. The handsome man offered to make copies of the research he and a friend had found and invited me to his library table. I thought, "Oh great now I don't have to spend a bunch of time finding articles and the friend probably was a girl." I was right on the first account, but wrong on the second account. The friend was a guy not a girl.

I found out the handsome man's name was Patrick and he was also smart. He offered his phone number to me just in case I had trouble writing my paper and I offered my phone number to him just in case he had a problem writing his paper. We both were flirting and having fun and then it was time for my evening class. I didn't like to miss class because I couldn't afford to get behind with my packed schedule. I said good bye and rushed off to class.

This is where Patrick and I differ on how this story goes. He believes I skipped class so that I could continue our flirtatious conversation. The truth is this: I went to the classroom and found a note on the door that said, "Class cancelled due to the professor's broken leg." I ran back to the library and reconnected with Patrick and his friend. Patrick invited me to grab a bite to eat and we quickly found a mutual attraction.

Our courtship began in March of 1987, a marriage proposal came in April, and we were married on December 19, 1987. It was a whirlwind time in our lives. We were considering eloping, but my mom insisted we get married in the Catholic church. My mother was skeptical of Patrick being my best-fit husband for several reasons. First, he was six years older than me and she had a misbelief that Patrick had been married before. She was also worried about Patrick's open confession of attending Alcoholics Anonymous and being clean and sober for seven years.

In hindsight, it was good we waited and took the premarital classes required for marriage in the Catholic church. I especially like the compatibility assessment we took and reviewed with a married couple from the church. The assessment pointed out our many common interests, common worldviews, and predicted a successful marriage.

We had a small Catholic wedding with immediate family and a few friends only, a lovely chicken dinner, and a Caribbean cruise honeymoon. The decision to have a small wedding offended some of our relatives but suited us just fine. I had to ask Patrick if we attended church the first few months after we got married because I couldn't remember. He thought we must have but wasn't sure. What does that say? I think it says that there wasn't a connection to the word of God or the congregation, just an obligation to check off each week.

"Search me, O God, and know my heart;
Test me and know my anxious thoughts." Psalm 139:23

MY BELOVED AND I

I can trace the beginning of my spiritual awakening to a Christian music rock concert in the Phoenix area. Patrick and I had completed our studies at The University of Michigan-Flint and we both earned teaching certificates. Teaching jobs were scarce in Michigan in the late 1980's. A University of Michigan instructor that Patrick had at that time told us about visiting Arizona and how there were new schools being built.

We thought, "Let's go there!" and we did. After being married for four months Patrick sold his little Sears bungalow in Flint and had his dad manage the rental house next door. We had some money from Patrick's buyout from General Motors, so we left with youthful enthusiasm and dreams of teaching.

We arrived in the Phoenix area in April of 1988 and I had just turned 25 years old. We managed to get part-time jobs while applying all over the state for teaching positions. I first worked in a car dealership as a receptionist. Ugh! It's true not to trust a used car salesman, at least at this dealership. I remember a young family looking at a white van to buy. While the family was outside the sales manager and other sales people were laughing at how they were going to overcharge the price of the van by thousands of dollars. This made me mad and disgusted and I quit shortly after that.

My next job was a seasonal one at a parks and recreation program. My duties included supervising elementary age children. It was almost teaching. I worked with this sweet woman who was an elementary school teacher. She was the one who invited Patrick and I to the Christian music rock concert. She gave me the address and time when to meet her and her husband at the concert. When we got to the address, I was surprised it was at a church. We never had music concerts, let alone rock music concerts, at the Catholic churches I went to.

This church was huge, white, and had modern architecture with auditorium seating. The band was set up in the front with a large bank of windows behind them. They started playing and song after song I became stirred up within me. I didn't recognize any of the songs, but with the lyrics posted on big screens I could follow along. People were standing, clapping, and had their hands raised in the air. I had seen hand clapping at secular music concerts, but all this joy and excitement about Jesus was foreign to me. I did a great deal of people watching that night. People were smiling and seemed genuinely happy to be singing about Jesus.

Close to the end of the concert a band member started talking while quiet instrumental music played in the background. His message went something like this:

"Do you have things you've done that you want to receive forgiveness for?"

"Do you believe Jesus, the son of God died on the cross to pay the price for your sins?"

He offered an invitation, "Come down and start a new life in Christ."

"Be forgiven and free"

"Just step out from your seat and come down to the front and start your relationship with Jesus"

People began to leave their seats. I watched. There were "helpers" at the front of the church who would talk to the people who had left their seats. This invitation was so encouraging, and I had that whole Gomer stage of my life that I needed forgiveness of. I so wanted to step out of my seat, but I was afraid, and I didn't budge. What would people think of me? Sadly, I rejected this invitation of salvation. It is the most regretful thing I can think of in my life. God was reaching down from heaven ready to exchange my box of stinky sin for a beautiful box of forgiveness, grace, mercy, love, and eternal life with Him in His Kingdom. If I only knew then what I know now.

This concert was the start of my spiritual searching. I felt a deeper need to solidify who I was, what I believed, my purpose and what this life is all about. You may be a 20 something year old or a 30 something year old and can relate to this deeper questioning I had. You may even be older and have the same yearning of purpose and meaning in your life.

What is different from the 1980's and 1990's, when I was a young adult, to the 21st century is the information and input overload. I had the television (that stopped broadcasting for 6 hours between the hours of midnight and 6:00am), magazines, books, and people in my life to listen and learn from. Now, there is 24-hour, 7 day a week availability of news, entertainment, and social connection to almost any part of the world. I find myself saying to people who want to know a fact or detail, "Just Google it."

A person can find information and "mis" information all day long which makes it easier to become more confused about the truth and what to believe. Also, there is much less down time for people now to process all this information to weed out fact from opinion. So, dear one, if you are on a spiritual journey like mine, you will have to be committed to unplugging from the barrage of voices and opinions to hear the truth of Jesus, *"I am the way and the truth and the life. No one comes to the Father (God) except through me." John 14:6.* God makes it so simple, there is only one way to Him. I hope, as you continue reading, you will receive and believe that Jesus is the way, the truth, and the life.

Life continued in the Phoenix area. I went on some teaching interviews. During one of them the interviewer asked, "What do you think of ESL?" I had no clue what ESL stood for and had to be honest. "I'm not familiar with ESL, but if I was I am sure I would have something to say about it." I answered.

The interviewer laughed and said it stood for English as a Second Language. As you can imagine, I didn't get called for a second interview.

However, a small school district in Northern Arizona did call and wanted to interview both Patrick and me! We got the atlas out, (no google maps or map quest back then), and found the small town where we were to report for our interviews. We added up the mileage and estimated a four to five-hour drive north from Phoenix.

Patrick said, "Maybe it's like Flagstaff. Remember how cool it was when we drove through it to get to Phoenix? Pine trees, mountains, and fresh air, I can see it now!"

The day we left for the interviews was full of anticipation. As we drove and drove and drove we went right past the pine trees, through the mountains, but the air stayed fresh. We ended up in the high desert with pinion bushes and the clearest blue skies I had ever seen, right on the southern border of the Navajo Reservation. The interviews went well, and we were hired on 8-8-88! I was to teach a multiage class of first, second, and third graders and Patrick was to teach high school Social Studies.

As we packed up and were preparing for our move up to the Navajo Reservation, Patrick's boss, from the community agency he had worked at helping the primarily disadvantaged Hispanic youth of Phoenix, invited us over for a send-off dinner. After the dinner, the hosts asked if they could pray for us. This was a first-time experience for us but wanting to be hospitable we allowed them to pray for us. As we sat together the two couples each put a hand on our shoulders. They took turns praying for our well-being, a positive teaching experience, God's protection, and for us to continue going to church. The two couples attended the Catholic Church, but they were not your typical Catholics. Later, in life, we found out they were charismatic Catholics.

Charismatic Catholicism is when churches place an emphasis on having a personal relationship with Jesus and express the gifts of the Holy Spirit in contrast to a traditional Catholic Church and Catholics.

The two years on the Navajo reservation were a culture change for us. We considered it our "domestic" peace corps experience. Ninety-Nine percent of the students we taught, and their families were Navajo. I learned so much about the native American life style and traditions, sometimes on purpose, mostly by accident. Like the first day of school, one of the third-grade boys in my class asked if he could make a "hogan" with the popsicle sticks I had put out on a table for free time.

"Hmmm," I thought, "What is a hogan?"

Out loud I said to the student, "What is a hogan?"

"You must not be from around here, Bellagona, hogans are our houses," giggled the student.

"Oh, then yes you can make a hogan," I replied.

"Boy, do I have a lot to learn and what does bellagona mean?" I thought.

I also learned that there are many Navajo superstitions. Like, if a coyote crosses in front of your path whether driving or walking, you must turn around and go back to where you started your journey otherwise you will have bad luck. Skin walkers were the "bogeymen" of the area and the children were scared with each tale about seeing them. Hogans all had their front doors facing the east because that is the direction of the rising sun. I also found out that bellagona was the Navajo word for a white woman.

Some traditional people went to the tribal medicine man to have a ceremony called a "sing" to help heal them of ailments. One day at school, one of my students raised his arms to stretch and his shirt went up to reveal white paint on his belly. I asked what the white paint was, and the boy and all the other children got big eyes and became totally silent. Finally, another student explained that there was a "sing" for the boy to help him get rid of the cold sores he was prone to get.

The only spiritual marker for us, from this time, was attending the small local Catholic church for a few months. We were asked to do the readings from the Bible. This was intimidating for me. What if I can't find the correct reading?

What if I read the wrong reading? What if I mispronounce a word? I didn't have to worry for long because Patrick wanted to attend an Alcoholics Anonymous meeting in a town forty miles away on Sunday mornings instead of going to the Catholic church. My spirituality became as dry as the desert we lived in at the time.

I kept busy with the rigors of being a new teacher, arriving an hour or so before the students and staying an hour or so after school dismissal. I had found my career calling as a teacher and I learned so much about the craft of teaching by attending many workshops and conferences, but I remained disconnected spiritually. Busy can stand for Buried Under Satan's Yoke. I interpret this as meaning being too full of activities and obligations that there is no time left in the day for pondering the deeper questions of life, reading the Bible or growing in a relationship with Jesus.

We moved back to the Phoenix area in 1990. My principal from the Navajo Reservation had moved to a school west of Phoenix and hired me to teach second grade. This makes 5 moves in 3 years of marriage.

THE SEARCH FOR IT

Moving and relocating became something we did a lot of over the past thirty years. It was at this time of my life that I started saying, "Is this it? If this is it, we need to make more of it." I felt like something major was missing in my life but didn't know what "It" was. I was so restless, and the search began for "It." You may be searching for "It," too. I hope you can learn from the dead ends I journeyed on to save precious time and energy.

I thought we needed more friends and social engagements. Maybe "it "was more relationships. I would arrange for Patrick and me to go out with my friends and their husbands and Patrick did the same with his friends and their wives. I learned an important lesson: just because the women were friends, or the men were friends didn't mean that the spouses were good fit friends.

We had some fun and funny times like the time Patrick and I went hiking with another couple. We had hiked this trail several times and this time Patrick suggested we go off the trail and blaze our own trail. I hesitated because it was posted in several places: DO NOT GO OFF THE DESIGNATED TRAIL. Patrick assured us all that it would be fine.

It started out fine with large boulders to sit on and views of beautiful vistas of the surrounding desert. It was very lovely until it was time to end our mountain hike. We had found a rocky ravine to make our descent and this is when it turned bad, bad, very bad. I went to take a step and almost stepped on a coiled-up rattle snake! Needless to say, I screamed my heart out. It scared the snake away, but Patrick and the others were dumbfounded as to why I was screaming, until they saw the snake I was pointing to because I was speechless. It got worse with every step. What we didn't know was this area of the mountain was off limits because of the large population of rattlesnakes that inhabited it, the reason for the many signs that said to STAY ON THE TRAIL.

With much fear and anxiety these thoughts were running through my mind, "What if someone gets bit? We are so far from any hospital. Are we all going to die?!" We made it safely down the mountain and out of harm's way. I am not so easily persuaded now to get off the trail since this incident.

Since more friends wasn't "It", maybe more activities or hobbies could be "It". I tried this route with country dance classes, sewing classes, gym membership, hiking, movies, biking, and reading. All of them fun and had some good benefits except the country dancing. The dance lessons were offered in a group setting with a couple as instructors. The class was titled a beginner's class, but we later found out that many of the couples had taken the class several times and were quite good dancers. Patrick claims I was too bossy, too mean, and I tried to lead all the time.

He said, "I quit!" and we never went back, and this was not "It."

Was "IT" more education? Patrick and I both pursued graduate degrees from Northern Arizona University. My Master's Degree was in Early Childhood Education. We spent two summers on the northern Arizona campus in Flagstaff. A fun time and reprieve from the heat, but not "It".

I tried finding "It" at the Catholic Church. Patrick and I attended each Sunday, volunteered to serve coffee and sweets after mass, and I almost joined the woman's group. These were not "It", however the teen mass on Sunday nights were engaging to me. The music was upbeat, the sermons had more life application and the teens performed different drama plays. This type of service was more of what I needed to get closer to "IT".

We started our trend of travelling early in our marriage. I love visiting new places. I tease that I must have some "gypsy blood" from my dad's side of the family, because of my desire to wander. I love the phrase "Not All Who Wander are Lost." Every time we travelled to a new place, whether it was a day trip, a weekend, or an extended stay, I would consider living there. Asking myself, "Could this new destination be "IT"?" I always came up with reasons for each place not to be "It". It's too dry, too wet, not enough trees, too busy, too slow, whatever the reason each place we visited had its uniqueness and fun, but each place was not "It".

Our most amusing, adventurous, and laborious trip up to this point was our 21-day tent camping trip from Arizona back to Michigan via California, Oregon, Washington,

Wyoming, and Minnesota. We were optimistic this budget-wise trip would be absolutely perfect. Patrick had plenty of camping experience. He loaded our little silver Dodge Omni with plastic milk crates that we "borrowed" from behind the school cafeteria up on the Reservation (or the "Rez" as it was locally known). There were camping pots and pans, a small gas cook stove, sleeping bags, a tent that was barely big enough for two people, and bicycles in a rack on top of the car.

The theme of the trip was realized very quickly as we left the desert state of Arizona. The theme was rain, rain, and more rain. It rained every day of our 21-day trip. We had become accustomed to the sunny days of Arizona and it never occurred to us to have alternative plans for the rain. Some days the rain was a mildly annoying drizzle and other days spotty showers and some days had complete downpours. The activities we planned were active outdoor activities; biking, hiking, swimming, and of course camping is outdoors. I'll share a couple of amusing highlights.

We were outside of Portland, Oregon camping at a state park. The park was known for the many waterfalls that could only be seen on the hiking trails. We had set up camp and started scoping out the trails on the trail maps. It happened to be only sprinkling that evening, so we were determined to hike to the waterfalls tomorrow morning no matter what the weather was.

As we awoke the next morning the rain was pouring on top of the tent and into the floor of the tent and there was thunder and lightning. It was so disappointing. I wish weather.com had been available back then because we would have hiked the evening before in the drizzle. Patrick and I looked at each other and said: "Let's just pack up and get out of here."

We stuffed wet gear into the hatchback of the car as quick as we could. I was trying to organize a few things in the hatchback and had my head tucked in the car to keep from getting too wet. Patrick didn't notice my head in the back of the car and grabbed the hatchback and tried to slam it shut. It banged the back of my head and brought me to tears. I was still crying from the bang on my head and the disappointment of the weather when I went to shower in the ladies bathroom. A concerned older woman asked me if I was hurt and I nodded. She assumed Patrick had intentionally hurt me and was ready to notify the authorities.

"No, no, no," I said, "He didn't hurt me on purpose. He accidently shut the hatchback on my head while we were packing in a hurry."

Thank goodness this satisfied her, and we had a friendly conversation about the local weather, rain and more rain.

We had managed to ride our bikes a little, hike a little, and meet some interesting people on this trip. We had made it to Minnesota and were anxious to get to Michigan to see family and sleep in a bed. Again, it rained while we slept in a Minnesota state park. When we woke up the rain had stopped, and I thought the tent had little sticks and leaf debris on it. I was sadly mistaken. Our tent was covered with all kinds of insects crawling all over it. The shower experience was even worse.

Patrick asked me, "Did you wear your "eyes" in the shower?"

Eyes referred to my contact lenses.

"No, "I answered.

"Good," said Patrick.

"What do you mean?" I asked wondering what he was getting at.

"The bathrooms were covered with cob webs and spiders," Patrick explained.

Traveling was and still is something we both enjoy, however I never found "It" on any trip.

FROM THE FRYING PAN TO THE FREEZER

Patrick and I had been in Arizona for seven years and it was March of 1995. March is what I refer to as my wiggly month. I get restless and some big life decisions have been made in March; meeting Patrick, deciding to move from Michigan to Arizona, and our decision to pursue teaching jobs in rural Alaska.

Yes, you read it right - rural Alaska, a move from the frying pan to the freezer. While I was teaching on the Navajo Reservation I went to a conference for teachers who taught in a multi-age classroom. I met a teacher from "the bush" in Alaska. The bush is any remote village in Alaska where access is by plane only. Alaska has a limited road system because of the diverse terrain. This teacher shared her experience and I was intrigued with the forty ninth state of the United States.

Originally, Patrick and I inquired about working as summer help at the Denali National Park. However, the requirements for seasonal work was being available from the beginning of May through September, not the period we had off as public-school teachers. This let-down led us to thinking of teaching in Alaska. Remember this is prior internet, so a phone call to the Alaska State School Board Office was the way to find out about teaching in Alaska. We were told there was a teaching job fair scheduled for the end of April with 100 job openings and approximately 200 people registered to attend.

We thought, "Hmmm, those are good odds for getting teaching jobs and they preferred teaching couples with different certifications to help with housing for teachers. Let's go for it!"

We were a bit impulsive and wrote letters of resignation to our principals before we even went to the job fair! Thank goodness my principal said he would keep the letter in his desk just in case this all didn't work out. We were very optimistic that we were Alaska bound. Patrick even sold all our furniture except a sofa sleeper and a television.

We had different spring breaks that year so while I was at school, Patrick emptied the contents from our furniture and had a furniture broker come and pick up the furniture. I came home that afternoon to find, what I thought was a ransacked condo! It looked like robbers had come in and stole all our furniture and left the stuff that was in drawers on the floor! I was freaking out, then Patrick came home and reported that we had not been robbed. He had sold all our furniture. It was a long three months with only that uncomfortable sofa sleeper and television.

We took four days off from school to fly up to Anchorage, Alaska, for the teaching job fair. We were giddy with excitement, but of course my excitement was more visible than Patrick's. The first thing we did when we got to the Captain Cook Hotel was to check out the room where the introduction meeting was to be held that evening. Well, our mouths dropped when we saw how big the room was and the abundance of chairs. I quickly counted the rows of chairs and the number in each row and multiplied—over 800 chairs! This was not what we had been told. We were initially discouraged, but an optimistic thought came to me, "Let's smile and go sell ourselves. We came here to get teaching jobs!"

Let me paint a picture of this job fair. The 800 applicants, all dressed in business attire, travelled to tables set up by school districts pitching their resumes. If an administrator from the school district wanted to have a more in-depth interview your name would be put up on a TV monitor with a time to report back to the school district's table.

This was 1995, before cell phones and the eve of the internet, so it sounds kind of primitive. Our names went up on the blue television screen several times. Each time we had to contain our excitement because we didn't know who was watching, perhaps a potential employer.

Our first job offer was a village on the very tip top of Alaska. The Superintendent who interviewed us was very honest, "The native people of the village won't like you, you'll have no running water, and by the way we have complete darkness for three months of the year, but the job is yours after you meet the President of the School Board." Lastly, he added, "You should wait for other offers before you make a final decision."

"Hmmm," I thought, "No running water for an entire school year, how does that work?"

That was when we learned about honey buckets and steam baths. Honey buckets, an ironic name for a five-gallon plastic bucket lined with a plastic garbage bag with a toilet seat attached to the top. Yup, that's right, you go to the bathroom in it and when it gets too stinky, you tie it up and put it outside in a 50-gallon metal barrel. The metal barrel has sharp triangle cuts in it, so the liquid can flow out and freeze until spring. I don't even want to think about the smell of the village come spring time.

If that's not enough to scare this ordinary gal away, the steam bath did the job. A steam bath takes place in a small wooden shed that has a metal tray of rocks inside that are heated by an outside fire. The heated rocks get water thrown on them to create steam and sweat. Several people, usually all males or all females, sit naked on wooden benches in the shed and sweat. Each person must bring a bucket of water, soap, shampoo, a wash cloth, and a towel. The individual buckets of water were for wetting hair, so it can be washed and rinsed and the same with the bodies. That just wasn't going to work for this shower girl. We put his offer on hold while we talked and interviewed with other schools from the Alaskan bush.

We started getting a little edgy because other teacher couples were getting hired. We knew this because the candidates' names were posted on the blue television monitors with the district name that hired them. We thought this would be a great time to pray so we quietly left the hotel and walked to the Catholic church just across the street. We sat in the silent church. My prayer was a prayer of desperation and went something like this, "God help us. We need these jobs since we have nothing to go back to in Arizona. Please send us a job offer soon." Sadly, this was the extent of the prayer; no thankfulness or praise to God, just an urgent request.

Patrick and I decided to find the school superintendent from the honey bucket and steam bath village and take him up on his offer. He was surprised we were back and reiterated the remoteness of the village, the substandard living conditions, and that the native people would try to run us out of the village. We were desperate and asked, "where do we sign our contracts?" He reminded us that we had to meet the school board president.

On the way down to meet the school board president. I started crying in the elevator. There were other people in the elevator, so we hurriedly got off the elevator and raced back to our hotel room. I broke down, "I can't do it! Not for a whole school year, maybe a weekend!" Patrick agreed and went to explain that while we appreciated the offer it wouldn't be a good fit for us. It was a nice vague explanation.

All was not lost though. Meanwhile, a school district that was less remote (although still accessed only by airplane), had running water (that had to be filtered to be potable) and never had complete darkness was interested in us. However, we had to leave on Thursday, a day before the job fair was scheduled to end with no offer of employment. We had met a teaching couple who were already working in "the bush" in the school district we were interested in. They were so informative about living and working with native Yupik Eskimos.

I remember flying back to Phoenix only a little disappointed because I knew we had given it our all. When we landed in Phoenix, Patrick went to a pay phone to check our answering machine remotely. The school district we were interested in had left a message offering us teaching positions in a small village 180 air miles southwest of Anchorage! We listened to the message twice maybe three times to make sure it was for real. We started hugging and jumping around the airport. We were moving to Alaska and with jobs! This would be move number 7 in seven years. This wasn't "It" but, it was a unique life experience. So, I will share the experience and the few spiritual markers I encountered along the way.

Our parents thought we were making a huge mistake. This wasn't the first time they thought this, and we sought encouragement outside our families. A teacher friend was extremely helpful and gave us several copies of the Alaska magazine and cheered us on as we prepared for the big move north to Alaska.

Since the village we lived in was not on the road system attending a local church was impossible. To accommodate the obligation for church attendance a priest named Father Kelly would fly into our village twice a month to conduct a Catholic mass at our house. He flew a little single engine plane in all kinds of weather; rain, snow, fog, sunshine, and cloudy. I remember one time when I brought him to the air strip to fly out of our village, the sky looked like a thick white blanket and I suggested he stay the night. He said it would be fine because there was a tiny ridge in the cloud that would enable him to make it above the clouds and fly home safely. He was very personable and if at any time I was going to find "It" in a Catholic church this would have been the time. I went through the mass sequence and said the prayers and even sang. Father Kelly said when we sang it was like praying twice, but I felt nothing spiritual. I was just fulfilling an obligation. I do remember lying in bed one night while still in Alaska thinking, "If I gave my whole life to Jesus there would be a whole lot of changes." After we had been gone from Alaska for about three years and living in Michigan, we got a phone call from a friend of Father Kelly's telling us that he had crashed his small plane into a mountain and perished.

The primary religion in the Alaskan village we lived in was Russian Orthodox. The church building was painted white and resembled a little old one-room school house with a light blue onion shaped steeple like the Russian spires in Moscow. Each grave in the small graveyard next to the church had the typical three-barred Russian Orthodox cross and a spirit house. A spirit house is a long low box with a peaked roof built over the graves. When I asked several natives what the boxes were for they would shrug it off and not answer. What I did find out on-line was that the spirit house was a native American tradition for the spirt of the dead person to have a place to live and not bother the living while it made its last journey.

Teaching and living in rural Alaska proved to be a cultural experience just like living and teaching on the Navajo reservation in Arizona was. Our school principal provided a family map of the three major families in the village of approximately 150 people. Almost everyone was blood related to each other or called each other cousin even if they were not related. "Confusing", to say the least. By the end of our 3 year stay, I finally could connect the dots to each of the family systems.

During our first year in Alaska there wasn't enough teacher housing for Patrick and me. The principal gave us the phone number of a native man who sometimes rented his cabin to teachers. There were no on-line pictures to see what the conditions of this cabin was, but we were assured it had electricity, heat, and indoor plumbing! While still in

Arizona finishing up the school year we made arrangements with this man to rent his cabin for the school year. He refused to take a security deposit, first and last month's rent, or have a signed rental agreement. This made us a little nervous at the time, but we later found out that's the Alaska way. Like when we made our flight reservations out to the village for the first time and the airline didn't require us to pay for our flights in advance. "Just pay us when you get to the airport."

It was a learning curve for living successfully in the bush. The teaching couple we met at the job fair was very helpful in sharing how they prepare to "go out in the bush" for the school year. With their recommendations and the checkbook, Patrick and I spent a week in Anchorage "bush" shopping. We purchased about 100 pounds of various bulk meat, which I packaged in smaller quantities in the hotel room and used the hotel freezer to freeze it. Most Anchorage hotels have freezers for guests to use for this purpose and to freeze fish and game that hunters had caught and wanted to bring with them back to the lower forty-eight. Then came the dry goods shopping. This consisted of finding the largest packages of products available, think of Costco. These goods along with hygiene products were boxed and mailed out to the village post office. The Anchorage post office is conveniently open 365 days a year 24 hours a day. The first time I saw someone put postage on a bulk package of toilet paper without a box was interesting, but it was a very common thing to see as we found out. The preparation week and bush shopping finally came to an expensive end. We thought we had bought enough food and supplies to get us to Christmas break, 4 months' worth.

The first part of the trip out to the bush was on a larger plane, about 48 passengers. The second part of the trip was much different, we had to take our first air taxi in a very small single engine plane. While the pilot was loading the building supplies for the remodel of the school where we would be teaching, the tail of the plane tipped backwards and touched the ground. I was concerned, very concerned, about the weight restrictions for the plane. I quickly shared our body weights with the pilot, so he could have a rough estimate of the total weight. The pilot added on our luggage, had us get in our seats and reassured us that everything would be fine. As we flew the 10 miles over the largest lake in Alaska to get to our new village, I couldn't help but think about the weight and the single engine. One engine problem and down we go! We didn't go down and crash even though we had heard several stories of other small planes crashing in rural Alaska.

The ride across the lake took about 15 minutes and was breathtakingly beautiful. We were so close to the lake water that we could see the waves. The small village of Kokhanok, Alaska came into view, along with the fuchsia flowered perennial plants called fireweed, that grew in abundance along the roads. The school was the largest building and was soon to be a little larger. The 25 or so houses were mostly shaped like shoeboxes on top of stilts. From the air all the little ponds and lakes looked like footsteps of a giant who had walked across this marshy land.

Before we landed, the pilot radioed the school that we were aboard as well as building materials. He instructed them to send the school suburban out to the air strip. It was all so exciting and dusty. All the roads in the village were either gravel or dirt with many ruts. The weather had been dry with little rain so whenever someone drove on the roads great clouds of dust followed behind the vehicle. We later learned that it was called getting "dusted." If you were walking and a vehicle passed by without slowing down to lessen the dust cloud, you would end up covered in dust.

When we landed the principal greeted us at the plane and told us that our many boxes that we had mailed were in the school gym and she told us she would take us to our little cabin in the woods. Finally, I would get to see our residence for the next school year. It was a little bit challenging getting to the cabin because of the rutted dirt roads through the woods.

The trees were mostly some kind of pine with gray fungus on the trunks and black moss on the branches that looked like hair. The Yupik Eskimo culture had their version of the bogeyman and it was named "hairy man." To them the black moss was evidence that he had been around.

Our cabin came into view, it was painted a barn red with a deck around most of the perimeter it included a garage and looked very quaint. It had an arctic porch, a kind of mudroom to put coats and boots, that prevented the cold outside air from rushing into the house when entering or leaving. It had a large living room with couches, a dining room with a table, one bedroom with a regular size bed, not the queen size I was told it would have. All in all, I thought it was going to be just great because it had indoor plumbing, heat, and electricity!

We had a week to get our cabin organized and our classrooms ready. This meant sorting through all the boxes, about 50 of them, that were in the school gym. Some went to the cabin, some to my classroom, and some to Patrick's classroom. My classroom was an old construction trailer next to the school, that had a deck built on to it. It did have its own bathroom and kitchen area and lots of voles. I had never heard of a vole until I came to Alaska. A vole is a small rodent, much like a mouse, but they have a reddish-brown coat of fur on their back. It became a graphing project with my students to see how many voles we could catch that first year. Every school morning the boys would run in to see if the trap that one of Patrick's students had set, had a dead vole in it or not. The graph topped out at 40 dead voles, ugh. Finally, the cold weather drove them underground for the winter.

I loved teaching in Alaska for many reasons. My little construction trailer classroom reminded me of a one room school house. I had kindergarten and first grade students in the morning and preschoolers in the afternoon. The children were eager to learn and did well learning to read with the phonics program, I brought with me from Arizona. My mom had sent up fabric and I sewed curtains for the classroom and a book bag for each student. They were encouraged to take a book home from school each night to read to their parents. Since I had the same students for the three years we lived in Kokhanok, I could see them mature and grow as competent students. *"Train a child in the way he should go, and when he is old he will not turn from it." Proverbs 22:6*

The Alaskan village we lived in used big diesel generators to power the electricity. When the school year finished in May, two of the three generators were turned off. This meant teachers had to leave the village in the summer. Patrick and I bought a truck and a over the cab camper and spent the summers traveling. We explored Alaska, drove the Alaskan Highway, and meandered back to Michigan to visit with family. We were able to meet many nice campers along the way and see the Canadian Rockies and the natural wonders of the western United States.

Another benefit from living in the bush in Alaska was the improvement in my cooking abilities. When Patrick and I married my cooking experience consisted of making sandwiches and salads. That was it. My sisters teased Patrick about starving to death because I couldn't even boil water. Patrick never starved to death and we are both well nourished. Patrick bought me cookbooks and I cut recipes out of magazines and gradually my cooking skills expanded.

There were no restaurants in our village which meant I cooked every meal. I planned monthly menus to help keep the meals varied and interesting. I burned out 2 bread making machines making sandwiches for our lunches, learned how to use powdered eggs and powdered milk and became a "professional" pizza maker.

Exercise in Alaska consisted of exercise videos, walking, hiking, and running. I loved hiking after a fresh snowfall. I recall one time on one of these hikes I stopped to rest on a snow bank. I laid back and looked up at the cloudy winter sky and heard nothing, absolutely nothing. There was no wind, no animal noise, and no vehicle noises. It was so amazing and peaceful. I later found out how uncommon it is to hear silence. *"Be still and know that I am God" Psalm 46:10*

AD : THE YEAR OF THE LORD

LOST BUT FOUND

Around Christmas time, during our third-year teaching in Kokhanok we decided to move back to Arizona. We were able to go back and teach for the same principals we had left to go and teach in Alaska. Life was good, but the search for "It" continued. I started listening to the Christian radio station, K-Love and I wore out an Amy Grant cassette. We went back to the same Catholic Church in Arizona. They had added a Sunday night service in the small chapel and we enjoyed the cozier setting.

I felt like it was time to move back to Michigan, but Patrick did not. We had some heated discussions about the topic. I reasoned that our parents were getting older and there were teaching jobs available in Michigan at the time. In March of 1999, we spent our spring break traveling around mid-Michigan peddling our resumes to principals. A bit unorthodox, but we were confident that our 11 years of varied teaching experience made us resourceful teaching candidates.

God worked it all out. We both secured teaching positions, sold our condo in Arizona, and moved back to Michigan that spring. We bought some property and Tom, my brother-in-law, supervised the building of our new home. It was a very busy time in our lives.

We moved into our newly built home on December 31, 1999. Yup, the eve of Y2K. If you are old enough, you probably remember the fear and chaos associated with the coming of the year of 2000. People predicted a meltdown in the infrastructure of the utilities like water, electricity and banking, all because of the unknown response of computerized systems and the date turning from the 1900's to the 2000's.

Patrick and I were so exhausted from the last six months of moving from Arizona, building a home, starting new jobs, and moving into our home. We didn't have many possessions so the move and unpacking that New Year's Eve was complete by early evening. I went to the grocery store to pick up a few items and it was practically cleared out of everything.

I thought, "Oh well, we will just have to beg and borrow from family and friends if this Y2K thing is for real." We feel asleep that night way before midnight in the living room watching tv. We said to each other, "If this is the end of the world at least we got to spend one night in our new house."

It was all good when we woke up around 2 am and the power was still on and we had running water. The whole Y2K doom of the end of our world as we knew it reminds me of people who get super consumed with the end times.

Many people through history have tried to predict the time and date when Jesus will return to earth, but all have been wrong. The Bible states, that *Jesus will return as a thief in the night. 1 Thessalonians 5:2*, meaning no one can predict the exact time, however the Bible also says to *"be ready, because the Son of Man will come at an hour when you do not expect him". Matthew 24:44*

We started attending mass at the Catholic Church I had attended with my family during my teen years. By this time, two of my nieces were in the teen group at the church. The group was planning a trip to Rome, Italy and needed extra chaperones. My sister Janet roped me into going. During the planning meetings, I felt the group, both the teens and the adults were not unified, on the purpose of the trip. Some were excited to meet the Pope, to others the city of Rome and the culture were intriguing, and just a few were interested in the spiritual or religious aspect of the trip. I had also developed mononucleosis at the end of the school year from trying to do everything in my own strength and was recovering over the summer.

The August 2000 mission trip was a challenge to say the least. I will just highlight a few of the major mishaps. The teens and some of the adults were violating the dress code in extreme ways, like thong bathing suits, for example. Factions of the large group decided to forego the planned schedule and do what they wanted, whenever they wanted, like going to bars and nude beaches. It was awful, and I felt a sense of responsibility to the parents of the teens since I was a chaperone.

We all survived, but a rift between my sister and nieces developed and was never quite resolved. Part of the trip really got me thinking; one of the activities during our 10-

day trip was to try and step through a designated number of cathedral doorways so you could be forgiven of your sins and go to heaven. I can't remember all the details, but it seemed like magical thinking or manmade thinking, and not from the Bible.

During the next two years the search for "It" surfaced again. We had settled down from the moving, the Rome trip, and our jobs felt more comfortable. Again, the spiritual truth, *"Be still and know that I am God." Psalm 46:10,* comes to my mind. Remember Satan's ways to interrupt our spiritual lives is to keep us busy (buried under Satan's yoke). When I have too many items on my list to do it overwhelms me. Before accepting Christ as my Lord and Savior, a good day for me was when I could check off and complete as many activities as possible each day. I would rise early, work hard, and drop into bed from exhaustion. However, I wasn't always able to fall asleep because my mind and body were over stimulated.

I searched again for "It" at the Catholic Church. I went back to what was familiar. I remember praying to God each Sunday, "God help me get something out of the sermon to use this week, so I can be a better person." I would listen and try to make a connection to my personal life, but nothing. I would sing the hymns and all I got were negative looks from the people sitting by me. I would look around for someone I knew or a friendly face to get to know to feel more connected. Nothing.

I recall on my way to work one morning, looking to the sky and saying, "What is the purpose of life? People are like scurrying ants all busy and for what?" I got this feeling that is hard to explain, like I was on to something big and it scared me. Could it have been God? Did my questions make him mad? I quickly started thinking about my list to do for that day and dismissed the whole thing.

Finally, I hit spiritual rock bottom and there was no place to go but up to God. It was a Sunday in the summer of 2002 and by this time Patrick had decided he would attend a Sunday AA meeting instead of going to the Catholic Church. This particular Sunday, I was very determined to get something to change my life from the service I went to, but it was the same as the past services, I got nothing! I got to my car and started crying. I was crying so hard I could barely see to drive home. I felt so hopeless, dry, and spiritually dead.

When I drove up the driveway Patrick was mowing the grass. I waved him down and when we got face to face and he could see I was crying. He asked, "What's wrong? Did something happen?" I blubbered back, "We're dead! Spiritually Dead! I don't get anything out of church and you don't even go to church! "

Patrick was a little disturbed by this revelation and my emotional outburst. Once he gathered his thoughts, he responded with, "How about we try Brandon's church?"

"Great, that's where we are going next week, together" I responded.

Brandon was an eighteen-year-old neighbor. There was something special about Brandon. He was polite, had a happy and pleasant disposition, and was wholesome. Both Patrick and Brandon worked building pole barns during the summer for another neighbor named Joe. One day when they were traveling to a job, Brandon pointed to the church he attended with his family. He invited Patrick to come and visit anytime. The church was a nondenominational community church with doctrine close to a Baptist church.

The next Sunday came. With great anticipation and excitement, I got dressed up, Patrick did too, and we set off for Hunter's Creek Community Church. Now, you must remember my history with the Catholic church to really understand the humor of the next narrative.

We walk in the doors and at once a smiling couple says, "Hello, Welcome to Hunters Creek Church. Are you visiting today?" I turn my head to look behind me thinking that this woman was talking to someone else. When I turned back around, I realized she was talking to Patrick and me. I was stunned. Someone was actually talking to me at church. This place was incredibly different than earlier church experiences.

This friendly couple introduced themselves and escorted us to separate Sunday school classes, one for men and one for ladies. This was the first time I went to Sunday school and felt welcomed right from the start. There were about 20 women and they were smiling and engaged in the teaching. I just sat and watched in amazement. After the class, Patrick and I met up and went into the sanctuary and were seated by more friendly people. As the singing began I looked around and did some people watching. People were singing and smiling, even the men! I nudged Patrick and whispered, "These people know something we don't know." I wanted to know what they knew because whatever it was, it was missing in my life.

Some more funny things happened at this new church on our first visit. The Pastor had asked the congregation to open their Bibles to a certain book and chapter. We didn't have Bibles but found some in the back of the pew in front us. Whew! But then I had no idea how to find the book and chapter the Pastor had requested. I thought to myself,

"There must be a table of contents or an index." I was getting nervous because as I looked around others had found the location and I hadn't. I noticed approximately where people had opened their Bibles, beginning, middle, or end of the book and started flipping the pages to that location. Thank goodness, I found the name of the book on the top of the pages and figured out from there how to find the chapter and verse. We never used the Bible in the Catholic church. The readings came printed in booklets called missalettes which led to zero knowledge of the Bible. Old Testament, New T estament, gospels, it was all foreign to me.

When the service ended, and people were leaving their pews the first couple we had met at the door asked us if we wanted to join them for lunch. What?! Not only was someone talking to us after church, but they wanted to get to know us too. It felt so welcoming and something that has become a common occurrence since we joined the family of God.

You might be thinking, "How does someone join the family of God?" I thought it meant church membership, but I was wrong. Joining the family of God can be easy as ABC. The A stands for admitting that you have sinned. *"For all have fallen short of the glory of God." Romans 3:23.* Sin is anything we think, say or do that is displeasing to God. Think of the 10 commandments. The B stands for believing that Jesus, the Son of God, died on the cross for the sin of the world and rose from the dead three days later to be seated at the right hand of God in heaven. *"Without the shedding of blood there is no forgiveness of sin." Hebrews 9:22.* The C stands for choose to confess this belief in a prayer. One church I attended has the whole congregation say a "Family Prayer" at the end of most services. It may vary a little bit each time, but it always has the ABC's. All the people attending the church service are asked to repeat the prayer section by section as the Pastor speaks it, even if you have already professed faith in Jesus Christ. It's a way of helping new believers feel more comfortable choosing to become a member of the Family of God.

Since I thought church membership was how to become a child of God, every time we attended Hunter's Creek Community Church I would fill out a visitor's card and mark that I wanted to become a member. After about two months the pastor called and asked if him and his wife could come and visit us at our house. "Yikes," I thought. "What could this be about?" The Pastor and his wife came over and used the bible to explain salvation, being saved, being born again, having a personal relationship with Jesus, asking Jesus into your heart, becoming a Christian, and joining the family of God, which all mean the same thing. I had heard about Jesus at the Catholic church and we said prayers about being a sinner, but it never seemed this clear before. Each person must choose to accept this gift of eternal life with God up in heaven and begin a personal relationship with Jesus through the Holy Spirit. I had to be born-again.

I finally found "IT"!! But "It" wasn't an it. "It" is this amazing relationship with Jesus Christ my Lord and Savior and friend. The people at Hunters Creek Community Church did know something we didn't know. It's called the full gospel, trusting Jesus to not only be fire insurance from going to hell when a person dies, but to guide us here on earth through the Holy Spirit, who indwells a person when they join the family of God.

Patrick and I, admitted being sinners, repented, and confessed our faith in Jesus Christ. We were baptized at Hunter's Creek Church in the fall of 2002. That was the start of our new lives in Christ. I thought I had a good life, but now I have an amazing life in Christ. *"I tell you the truth, no one can see the kingdom of God unless he is born again." John 3:3*

REFINEMENT

In the book, <u>Unlimiting God</u>, Richard Blackaby, the author writes a word picture that he titles Mountain Climbing.

"Each person who becomes a Christian is like someone who's invited to climb a majestic mountain. People respond differently to such a glorious opportunity. Some never leave the foot of the mountain. They gaze up at its grandeur and feel overwhelmed and inadequate to take on such a challenge. So, they remain where they are."

Richard goes on to say how some begin the journey, but slow down and eventually stop climbing from lack of motivation, grumbling and complaining, and conflict. "But a handful of dedicated and determined hikers continues to move upward, each one at his or her own pace."

Mountain Climbing is concluded with this, "Knowing the Lord is like climbing that mountain. The ascent is available to all, but not everyone reaches the same level. Each of us decides how much effort to expend to reach the heights; each of us ultimately decides how far and how high we'll go."

I have twice read this book, Unlimiting God, and feel this passage has had a strong impact on my spiritual growth. I want to be the hiker on the mountain who keeps going higher and deeper with my walk with Jesus.

I came to my personal relationship with Christ at the age of 39. Initially this was very discouraging to me and I would think things like:

"How come nobody told me about trusting Jesus as my Savior?"

"Were all the people I have met thus far in my life lost, too?"

"How come it took so long for me to hear the Good News?"

These discouraging thoughts brought me down, but as I took hold of the fact that the opportunity to grow in relationship to Christ is limitless, the discouragement of my midlife conversion passed away. Whatever age you are, you too can be saved from a life lost to sin and emptiness and be brought into the abundant life with Jesus, the Son of God.

The next fifteen years were a time of spiritual growth. Both Patrick and I were hungry to learn more about being born again and about Jesus Himself. I feel so grateful that both Patrick and I professed faith in Jesus Christ at the same time. We would talk about sermons, read the Bible and have discussions, and helped each other be accountable to the Word of God.

I know women who have unsaved husbands and it can be difficult. When a person asks Jesus into their life, as Lord and Savior, they are a new creature and are filled with joy about their decision. They want to talk about God and all the new revelations about life. In 1 Corinthians 7 Apostle Paul gives instructions on Christian marriage. Verses 14 and 16 give us much hope, *"For the unbelieving husband has been sanctified through his wife, and the unbelieving wife has been sanctified through her believing husband. Otherwise your children would be unclean, but as it is, they are holy." "How do you know, wife, whether you will save your husband? Or, how do you know, husband, whether you will save your wife?"*

God, through the Holy Spirit, had a great deal of work to do correcting all the misconceptions I had about living life. The Holy Spirit is the inside guide for all believers. When a person believes that Jesus is their Savior the Holy Spirit is deposited within the person's spirit. This is where being "born again" comes from. We are not physically reborn, but God's spirit is now joined to our spirit. It is a marvelous mystery!

In Sarah Youngs book, *Jesus Calling*, she has written about this mystery so beautifully as if Jesus himself is explaining this amazing fact;

"I am Christ in you, the hope of Glory. The One who walks beside you, holding you by your hand, is the same One who lives within you. This is a deep unfathomable mystery. You and I are intertwined in an intimacy involving every fiber of your being. The light of My Presence shines within you, as well as upon you, I am in you and you are in Me: Therefore, nothing in heaven or on earth can separate you from Me!"

I love this promise that God will never leave one of His children nor forsake any of them. I take comfort knowing I am never alone whether I am living in good times or hard times.

I have heard this saying, "God loves us right where we are at, but He loves us too much to let us stay there." I am not sure who to give credit to for this wise statement, but I am grateful for it. My interpretation is that God loves all people regardless of their status, past actions or decisions, so there is no need to "clean yourself up" before accepting the grace and mercy that God offers. However, after a person trusts Jesus to be their Lord and Savior, God will change and refine a person to be a better reflection of Himself. *"This third I will bring into the fire: I will refine them like silver and test them like gold." Zechariah 1:9*

This is a life-long process compared to the refining of precious metals. Silver and gold are heated to high temperatures to melt the metal into a liquid. The impurities in the metal float to the top and are skimmed off. God considers us even more important than these precious metals and will turn up the heat to rid us of our impurities. Some of the refinement God put me through was easy. I was already a nonsmoker and nondrinker and rarely said a swear word so these were easy. Rubbing off my pride in my career was a much more difficult task.

I had been teaching for 11 years and had developed what I thought was confidence in my teaching abilities. Patrick and I had moved back to Michigan and started new teaching jobs. The elementary school where I was hired to teach was only a year old, set in a country setting, and was in Michigan. I was so excited to be teaching in my home state of Michigan. We had spent two years on the Navajo Reservation in Arizona, six years in the Phoenix area, three years in the Bush in Alaska, and now home in Michigan, again. Can you tell I was extremely excited to be back in Michigan?

Competition in the work place is common and teachers can be very competitive. Also, many people are resistant to change. I came to find out, bit by bit, how an "old guard" was in charge at the elementary school. This "old guard" was comprised of teachers who had lived in the community, some for their entire life, who had a critical spirit. This critical spirit, I later found out, was a way to mask their insecurities.

It seemed that this quaint little elementary school was in a time warp. Some of the classrooms looked like a step back to the early 1970's when I attended elementary school. Since I had taught in several diverse communities and was blessed to receive a great deal of professional development through workshops and a master's degree, I had a few different ideas about teaching young children. The "old guard" was not accustomed to a newbie coming in with new ways and this caused friction.

I didn't set out to have this conflict with the "old guard," but I also didn't succumb to their negative authority. Instead, I taught with gusto, kept going to workshops, was asked to join school leadership committees, and tried to share teaching strategies with other teachers. I was there to teach children, not worry about co-workers. This strategy left me with a grumbling attitude about the "old guard."

There were three pivotal situations during this time that changed my grumbling attitude. The first was being invited to be a part of an after-school Bible club for elementary students called, "The Good News Club." I had been saved for about a year when a parent of a student from the class I taught the previous year, approached me with the opportunity. We had some small talk then she said, "I would like to invite you to help at The Good News Club we have at the school."

I asked, "What's The Good News Club?"

She proceeded to tell me about the Bible club that was comprised of a Bible story, memory verse, singing, games, and a snack. It sounded interesting, but I felt a little nervous about church and state issues. "You'll have to get some training and it's starting in a few weeks. Are you interested?" She asked.

"Well… How did you come to ask me to help with The Good News Club?" I answered back with a question. She said, "I prayed about it and God revealed your name."

"What!! God can do things like that?" I asked

"Yes, He can!" she excitedly answered.

"I just got saved a little while ago, so this is all new to me." I said

With a tear in her eye she quietly said, "I knew you were different." She never did tell me exactly what was different about me.

I took the training and it was just what I needed. Even though I was a forty-year old woman I was considered a baby Christian. Baby in the sense that I had to be taught and learn about God, so I could understand the love of God. The Bible verse that was most memorable from the training was, *"Keep your lives free from the love of money and be content with what you have, because God has said, 'Never will I leave you; never will I forsake you'." Hebrews 13:5.*

Contentment, for me, comes when I trust God more and more for all my needs. A person may walk away from God, but God is so faithful, He will never leave us. I also found this verse in *Psalm 9, "Those who know your name will trust in you. For you, Lord, have never forsaken those who seek you."*

I love how God has purposely repeated important promises in the Bible to help believers never forget how wide, deep, and long His love is for us.

I served a few years in The Good News Club and many children came to The Lord. Some teachers said negative things about a church activity taking place in a public school and I got fearful. I quit serving because I believed Satan's whispers about the possibility of a conflict with the separation of church and state. I have regretted this action and hoped to be active in a Good News Club in the future. Since moving to Florida God has ordained just that! I am part of a team who proclaims the Gospel of Jesus Christ in The Good News Club at a local elementary school. God is so good!

The second way God helped me see His heart, during this lengthy refinement period, was when I participated in a women's Bible study called, Apples of Gold. This was an awesome experience for me. More mature Christian women were mentors and myself and others were the mentees. For six weeks we met for a cooking demonstration, a Biblical topic of study and a meal. One week I was complaining about my work situation; "people don't want to work together, some people refuse to try new ideas, I'm only trying to help the children, blah, blah, blah." At this point in my career I was a school counselor and playing a big role in implementing an initiative for positive behavior and reading support.

The next time we met for Apples of Gold Bible study the pastor's wife told me this, "I was thinking about what you shared last time and I have a verse for you to look up and contemplate."

Philippians 2:3-4 "Do nothing out of selfish ambition or vain conceit, but in humility consider others better than yourselves. Each of you should look not only to your own interests, but also to the interests of others."

While meditating on this passage of Scripture, I had a lot to think about; "Was I all about selfish ambition? Was I only thinking of myself? Did I even listen to others concerns?" It didn't happen overnight, but that verse has helped me become more and more Christlike. Jesus, who is the true example of humility, has shown me His perspective. He loves all people and wants each one to believe in Him and to be the best version of their individual selves.

The competition, comparing, and critical spirit I had, had to go. I thought the coworkers that were difficult to work were my enemies and I wanted God to teach them a lesson, but I was the one being taught the lessons! It's amazing how learning about God's perspective, praying for God's perspective, and looking at life from God's perspective can make *all things work for the good of those who love Him. Romans 8:28.* I love God and He was using these difficult situations to refine me so He could use me to further His kingdom. I wasn't particularly useful when all I was doing was complaining and grumbling.

The third refining situation occurred after a day of team building with the teaching staff. An outside consultant came in for the day to guide us in many worthwhile activities: determining our personality types, how to appreciate each different type, and we played team building games. I approached the consultant privately, to ask for suggestions on how to mend a broken work relationship with a specific individual. She suggested asking the person outright, in private, what's wrong and that you're willing to work together to fix it. "Eeesh!" I thought. "That sounds simple enough and easy enough in theory and being alone with an enemy sounded downright scary. But if it will make things better I will try it."

So not to lose my courage, the very next morning before school started, as this teacher was walking past my classroom, I invited her into to my classroom. I started off by sharing how the consultant from yesterday recommended talking it out with people we are having conflict with.

Next, I asked her, "How come we don't get along?"

To this very day, I am shocked by her response. "It's you," she said with a shaky and tearful voice, "You think only your ideas are great and that none of us have good ideas."

She always appeared so strong and opinionated that I didn't think anything could ruffle her feathers. I had been so wrong about her. She wasn't an enemy, she was a wounded woman who used a tough exterior to cover it up.

"I'm so sorry," I said, "I don't think only my ideas are great. I just like to share ideas and strategies that I have found to work well with kids."

"Well that's not what it feels like," she said and huffed out of my room with tears streaming down her face.

Unfortunately, we never did finish that conversation or come to any kind of resolution between us, however it had a profound effect on me. This experience opened my mind and heart to look deeper and beyond a person's exterior behavior. I have come to believe easily angered, annoyed, and aggressive people use these behaviors to mask or cover up their insecurities or woundedness. When I have encountered such people, I tend to back off and leave them alone, which makes their tough exterior a useful self-defense mechanism to keep others away. This isolation hinders addressing the root of their negative behavior. We all have insecurities and woundedness and a personal relationship with Jesus Christ is the only way to have lasting healing and to become the best version of ourselves. *"Show me your ways,*

O Lord, teach me your paths; guide me in your truth and teach me, for you are God my Savior, and my hope is in you all day long." Psalm 25:4-5

PREPARATION FOR ASSIGNMENTS

I mentioned in the introduction how writing this book about the relationship I have with The Extraordinary God was an assignment from God. The concept of an assignment from God comes from the many years I was a teacher. As a teacher I assigned many assignments to students. I had the expectation that each student would accept and embrace the assignment and complete it to the best of their ability using the information and content that I had previously taught them. There were many purposes for these assignments: check for understanding, check for mastery, engage my students with the information they had learned, build a strong work ethic, and sometimes to keep them engaged while I worked with individual students. When I evaluated these assignments, it would help me to know if the students mastered the teaching objective or if they needed more practice.

Now let's put these assignment concepts from my teaching years together with the ways of God. God longs to be our Heavenly Father and to help us learn and grow in His ways. Just like an earthly father, but better, God teaches us, helps us mature, and disciplines us. God does His teaching through the Bible. I have learned so much about God by reading the Bible, participating in Bible studies, and listening to sermons either at church or on an electronic device. God checks our understanding of Him through assignments just like an earthly teacher. Assignments from God come through the Holy Spirit. For me, it's a command to do something that I heard or was shown to my spirit.

When I was first born again these commands were confusing to me. I didn't know if it was me and my own thoughts or the voice of the Holy Spirit. I would say something like, "God, is that your idea or my idea?" For many of God's first assignments I did nothing because I wasn't sure it was the Holy Spirit communicating with me. I remember mentioning this to a Christian friend and asking her, "How do you know who's doing the talking." She really didn't have an answer and kind of looked at me weird.

What I have learned since then is quite amazing. As I learned about God in the Bible, praised and prayed, and spent time meditating on God's ways. Then a personal relationship developed between God and me. I was given discernment to recognize Him through the voice of the Holy Spirit. I remember praying for the eyes and heart of God, I prayed for God's wisdom, I praised God, I asked for help to do God's will, not mine. These verses were especially important, and I wrote them several times in my journals:

"Direct my footsteps according to your word, let no sin rule over me."
Psalm 119:133

"Make your face shine upon your servant and teach me your decrees."
Psalm 119:135
"Show me Your ways, teach me Your paths;
Guide me in Your truth and teach me,
For You are God my savior,
And my hope is in you all day long." Psalm 25:4-5

Over time, about 8 years, I started to hear assignments, without a doubt, knowing God was using the Holy Spirit to communicate with me. God had heard my prayers and answered them as I showed maturity in His Ways.

One of the biggest assignments I have had was when my mother was living in an assisted living facility plagued with the memory disease of Alzheimer's. It was the summer of 2011 and I was off from teaching for my summer break. My usual summer work was to keep our 14 or so flower beds weed free. I called it "the war on weeds". That summer, my weeding work was interrupted by an assignment from God. The assignment I felt from God was this, "If you want to do anything with your mom, you better do it quickly because her time is running out." With this assignment came a vision of this big burgundy colored wall clock that we had hanging in the basement. This clock image came to me over and over that summer.

My mom had signs of memory problems for several years, however she hid them well. She insisted on living alone which prevented anyone from knowing her strange sleep habits, taking double or triple dosages of her medications, and getting lost while driving in the small town we all lived. All of this was pieced together by my sisters and I as we shared our individual experiences with my mom over her last years. Her official diagnosis came from an emergency room visit when my mom was convinced I was missing.

77

It was a Saturday morning in May of 2010 and I stopped by my mom's house. She was napping on the couch; the couch had all the cushions removed because she was washing the covers. The whole living room was in a disarray and her explanation for the mess was she was spring cleaning. The curious thing was what she said to me when I woke her up, "Oh hi, how was your trip to the cabin?" I responded, "What cabin? I just came from church." I figured she must have been dreaming and that was part of the dream, but no, she was adamant that I had been at the cabin. We didn't have a cabin, nor did we ever have a cabin. After disagreeing for a few minutes, she got up and huffed off into the kitchen. I thought, "That was weird."

I helped her get her living room back in order and invited her to come to my house for a late lunch. My inlaws were also going to be there, and she liked visiting with them. We used to joke about who talked the most, Harrold my-father-in-law or my mother. She accepted the invitation and showed up close to the scheduled time. My mother was notorious for being late.

After we ate inside we went to sit on the front porch. My mom started to perseverate on her purse, which she had left in her car. She said, about 20 times, "Where's my purse?" with a look of fear that she had left it someplace. One of us would respond, "You left your purse in your car." She would calm down and would be satisfied with the answer for a short period of time then ask again, "Where's my purse?"

My in-laws, Patrick, and I gave each other looks of concern and shrugged shoulders. I thought, "This is weird and wrong. I need to talk to my sister Janet about this." Janet and I had suspected something was off with my mom and decided to use the month of May to visit my mom more and get more insight into the situation.

I got to talk to Janet at about 2 am that night. What we pieced together with the help of the police was this: After my mom left my house she went home. Later in the night around 11:00PM she called 911. She told the police that her daughter, Jill was missing. She told them I was there with a friend to spend the night and when she went to check on us we were gone.

The police arrived at my mom's house to find her in her nightgown all wet from being out in the rain looking for me. The police were confused because they thought they were coming out to look for a missing minor child, not an adult child. One of the police officers noted the names on my mom's phone and asked about them. My mom said those are my daughter's names. The police officer called Janet's number and asked her to come over to my mom's house because of the confusing incident.

When Janet and her husband Tom arrived, the police said this happens with older people and sometimes their blood sugar is too high or too low. Janet checked my mom's blood sugar and it was normal. However, they still weren't sure if I was really missing, and clarify that I was not a minor, but a 47-year-old married woman. My sister tried calling me several times, but I never answered. Note to self: Don't leave your cell phone in another room on vibrate at night. Finally, my brother-in-law drove over to our house at 2AM to see if I was there. The doorbell jarred me awake and I woke Patrick up and we both went to the front door. We were very surprised to see Tom and even more surprised to hear what was happening at my mom's.

The police recommended that we take our mom to the emergency room for a complete evaluation. We took mom to the ER and they confirmed the dreadful diagnosis of Alzheimer's. The question from the evaluation that stands out to this day in my mind was when the neurologist asked my mom, "How many daughters do you have and what are their names?" My mom chuckled and said, "Now you are trying to give me a trick question? I don't have any daughters." I interjected, "Mom, yes you do. You have 4 daughters and their names are Jenifer, Janet, Jill, and Jackie." This got my mom's attention and she looked at me with a perplexed look, like she was trying to put the pieces of her life together. She finally responded with, "Oh yeah, I have 4 daughters."

I had brought my Bible to the hospital that night and this was the scripture I was reading from

"God is our refuge and strength,

An ever-present help in trouble.

Therefore we will not fear, though the earth give way…" Psalm 46:1-2

Be still, and know that I am God; Psalm 46:10

God knew just what I needed to hear from Him in the dim light of my mother's hospital room. I heard God is my eternal refuge and He is always there to provide strength, security, peace, and help for those who love Him. I prayed, "I love you God and I need you." The dismal prognosis of my mother's disease kept me close to God. *"Because (s)he loves me, says the LORD, I will rescue him(er); I will protect him(er), for (s)he acknowledges my name."* Psalm 91:14

GOD'S ASSIGNMENTS

My usual visitation schedule for my mom during the school year was Wednesday evening and Sunday dinner at my sister Janet's house. This changed drastically after accepting God's assignment. That summer I went to visit my mom about three times a week along with the Sunday dinner. I would try to take her out for mini-field trips. She thought the small town I would take her for coffee and a sweet treat was the town she grew up in and I went along with it. It made her happy to reminisce about her early years. Being able to recall old long- term memories is quite common for patients with memory loss. There were some humorous events during these outings.

Two that are seared into my memory both have to do with bathroom mishaps. The first was when I had my mom out for coffee and a sweet treat, and since this was our coping mechanism I packed on some pounds during this time. We were getting ready to leave and go to a small vegetable stand I saw on the way to the bakery. I told my mom to use the bathroom before we left the bakery. She assured me that she didn't have to use the bathroom at the time.

So... we left and went to the vegetable stand. While we were picking out some tomatoes my mother informs me, "I have to use the bathroom." "What!?," I said, "How come you didn't use the bathroom at the bakery? There are only porta-potties here." I think you can imagine the dilemma that ensued. We both went in, so I could keep reminding my mom not to touch anything and not to sit on the seat. However, to not sit on the toilet seat, my mom grabbed the urinal to steady herself. Ugh, I was so disgusted, and my mom was completely fine.

The second memorable event happened near the end of my summer break. It was a hot and humid Sunday. I thought taking my mom to one of Michigan's great lakes would be a refreshing way to spend the afternoon. Patrick had a bad feeling about this idea. He said, "It's a long drive. Will your mom really enjoy it? Let's just go visit her and call it good." The image of the clock ticking away came to me and I wanted to know that I had taken every opportunity to be with my mom doing fun things. I talked Patrick into the outing and at first it was fine. The drive went well, and we found a restaurant to have lunch. As we parked and got out of the car, the heat and humidity hit us square in the face. It wasn't cooler at the lake. It was hotter and there was no breeze. The original plan of getting take out and having a picnic was scratched. "Oh well, we can still eat inside and walk along the pier afterwards." I thought.

In the restaurant, my mom said she needed the restroom. I went with her but didn't realize she now needed assistance with this activity. When she tried to sit on the toilet seat she missed and fell to the floor with a thud. I quickly asked her, "What happened mom? Are you ok?" She was dazed and mumbled something I couldn't understand. I bent over and looked under the stall and saw my mom sitting, bare-bottomed, on the public bathroom floor!

At first, I was immobile not knowing what to do. Then I heard the Holy Spirit say, "DO SOMETHING, YOU'RE IN CHARGE." That put me into action and I crawled under the stall and heaved my mother, who thankfully weighed only about 100 pounds, up onto the toilet seat. With perspiration dripping from my hairline and shaking a little bit I asked my mom again, "Are you ok? Do you hurt anywhere?" She responded, "I'm fine." Like falling on a public bathroom floor was an everyday occurrence.

Since this bathroom visit took a long time, Patrick began to wonder about us. When we finally made it back to the table after trying to degerm my hands and arms and my mom's hands and arms. Patrick gave me a raised eyebrow and shrug of the shoulder. I said, "Don't ask. I can't even think about it right now. I'll tell you later."

By the end of summer our excursions had to be discontinued. I was back in school and my mom's condition had deteriorated to the point that she now was only able to get out for Sunday dinners at my sister's house. The fall season was very depressing with further cognitive decline and the loss of bodily functions. Going to see my mom became more difficult. I would work at school until about 6:00PM, then visit for a short period of time. Having a loved one with a memory disease gave me such a defeated and helpless feeling. The physical part of my mom was there, but the social and emotional part had drifted away. My mom had the gift of gab and even that disappeared.

My mom died on December 18, 2011, just six months after I was given the assignment to spend more time with her. I took a walk the day after she died, and the sun rays were shining down on me brightly, even though it was a December day in Michigan. I felt God say, "Good job and you are decommissioned from this service." It felt so wonderful, beyond wonderful, to have listened and obeyed. I will always treasure the happy memories of visiting with my mom and taking her on short fieldtrips.

Recently, I have had assignments to go and talk to certain people, sometimes it's a person I know and sometimes a person I have never met. I know they are assignments from God because of the persistence of the request and the challenge of the assignment for me to step out of my comfort zone and talk about Jesus.

One assignment happened on a work morning. My morning routine was bible reading and study, breakfast, and going for a bike ride. Then I had to quickly get ready for work and leave. This particular morning was cloudy and there were a few sprinkles. I took the risk of biking in the sprinkles. As I was concluding the ride I made my way through the parking lot of the apartment complex where we lived. There was a woman in a green car waving at me. I didn't recognize her but waved back anyways.

In a matter of a few minutes I had put my bike in the garage and was walking inside to get ready for work when I heard, "Go talk to that lady. She's a Jesus Girl too." "What!? I thought, "I don't know her and besides I have to get ready for work." I walked up a few of the steps to our second-floor apartment. Then I heard again, "Go talk to her." I sensed some type of urgency and turned around, went outside, and walked to her car. She rolled down her window and said, "Not very good weather to be on a bike ride."

I responded, "Yeah, I just needed some exercise before I go to work and by the way are you a Jesus Girl?"

She looked surprised then happy and said, "I am."

I explained to her how God had prompted me to come over and talk to her and she did indeed talk. In a matter of about 5 minutes she shared her distress about finding a job, her custody battles with her ex-boyfriend, and immigration problems. She was talking a mile a minute and I asked her to stop. I said, "This spirit of confusion you're having is not from God." She was silent and staring at me. Then she said, "Thank you, I needed to hear that because I get overwhelmed with my circumstances and then paralyzed with fear."

I had a few suggestions for job possibilities, told her to pray. I should have prayed with her but didn't. I excused myself and walked away thinking, "I'm not sure what just happened, but it was great! Thank you, Jesus!" With prompting and help from the Holy Spirit I have found a new boldness to step out and talk about Jesus and share with others the hope and wisdom that comes from being in a relationship with Him. *"For we are God's workmanship, created in Christ Jesus to do good works, which God prepared in advance for us to do." Ephesians 2:10.*

SURRENDER: END OF SELF - INTO GOD'S WILL

My long season of refinement with work pride came to an end in my first-grade classroom. It was March 2014. I got on my knees on the blue story-time carpet, with my elbows on the purple stool, where I sat to read stories to the children and cried. I then raised my arms up high and cried out to God, "God, I have nothing left, the kids will be at the classroom door in less than 5 minutes and I'm not ready for the day and I would rather walk out the door and go home. Help me Lord!" My prayer of surrender was the open-door God needed to help me get closer to His promise that it is His Power and Strength that allows me to do all things. It is not my own will power and strength because I had run that tank empty. There were no more "big girl pants" in the closet to put on. No more umph. I was burned out. It was scary, but a necessary place to be, for God to move in to be Lord of my life.

The burnout symptoms I had were anxiety, depression, and irritability, feeling tired even after resting, and feelings of ineffectiveness and lack of accomplishment at work. The stress from caregiving, grief, work, and menopause had all compounded together and left me overwhelmed.

That school day went well under the power of Christ, but it's what happened during the month after that prayer of surrender that is amazing. I had the dream of using my counseling degree to counsel children in a clinical setting. Patrick was always against this idea for financial reasons. He would say things like, "You would be starting a brand-new career at the bottom of the pay scale, you're used to making such and such amount of money, it won't work, it's a bad idea." I would listen to him on the surface, then tuck this dream away for another time not knowing that God was already at work. The verse, *"Delight Yourself in the Lord and He will give you the desires of your heart." Psalm 37:4* came to mind as I was writing this.

I had made a commitment to read the Bible every morning since September 2009. This meant getting up to the alarm at 4:45 AM on school days. At this point in time, daily Bible reading and prayer had become a five-year discipline which had drawn me closer to the ways of God. *"In the morning, O LORD, you hear my voice: in the morning I lay my requests before you and wait in expectation." Psalm 5:3*

During the summer of 2013 I worked on upgrading my counseling license from a Limited License Professional Counselor to a Licensed Professional Counselor. This upgrade was needed to work outside the school setting in a counseling position. It was quite a process; national test, fingerprinting, state application, and signatures from supervisors. I studied for the test all summer and was scheduled to take the exam in August. I read test prep questions, listened to cd's about the test while driving and doing housework, and prayed. My prayers were for the information I was studying to be put into my long-term memory and easy to recall and to have the mind of Christ for the many ethical scenarios included in the exam. I was in a neighborhood afternoon ladies Bible study and asked them to pray for a good outcome too.

The test location was at an H and R Block office, strange location to me, but also great because after completing the exam an immediate print out of my results were available. After several hours of reading and answering questions on a computer screen, not my favorite way to read, I passed the national exam. The passing exam score document was the last requirement needed to be a certified Licensed Professional Counselor! But now what?! I felt this sense of urgency all summer to complete the process for my counseling license, then I was confused because I wasn't changing careers because Patrick wasn't in agreement.

That summer, I had been researching mental health clinics in the area where I lived and even drove by some of them. I had my heart set on one, which was connected to the local hospital and had a large staff of 4 psychiatrists and 20 therapists. I knew this because I had previewed their website many times and read every clinicians biography. I shared all this information with Patrick. Again, he did not share my enthusiasm for a career change.

The school year started and one day early on, as I was stopped in my vehicle getting ready to turn left out of our subdivision to go to school, I hear The Holy Spirit say, "One day you will turn right to go to work not left." "Huh?!" I thought, "That would be a long way to get to school or that is the way to the counseling clinic I had researched during the summer." I tucked this information in my heart and pondered it, telling no one at the time about it. *"But Mary treasured up all these things and pondered them in her heart."* Luke 2:19

I have found, in my life, God works in subtle ways and if I am too busy or distracted I don't hear the voice of the Holy Spirit. This time I was positive I heard what I heard.

The school year trudged on. At Christmas break, while visiting family in Florida I prayed The Prayer of Jabez.

"Oh, that you would bless me
and enlarge my territory!
Let Your hand be with me,
And keep me from harm
so that I will be free from pain." 1 Chronicles 4:10

The Bible says that *"Jabez was more honorable than his brothers." 1 Chronicles 4:9* and that he was remembered for this prayer not a heroic act. Jabez asked that God bless him, help him in his work, be with him in all he did, keep him from evil, and that he be kept from harm and he wouldn't harm anyone. I was asking God to enlarge my territory in my line of work not really knowing what that would look like, but knowing I needed something fresh.

A week or so after the day of surrender I was at a teacher's conference. I left the conference with a heavy heart and felt led to stop at a school in my hometown where I kind of knew the principal. The principal had been a guest speaker in one of my counseling classes when I was getting my master's degree. She had an interesting career path: special education teacher, school counselor, principal, building administrator, and she also had a pet therapy dog. She agreed to meet with me and I shared about my need for a change and she listened. She encouraged me to send my resume to her with no promise of any job. I updated my resume and sent it to her and never heard a thing from her. But taking the time to update my resume was essential in what happened next.

Shortly after that day, Patrick came home from school and said, "Hey, I was at a county-wide school counselor's meeting today and I talked with Amy. She used to work at the clinic you're interested in working at and her husband, Bill, works there now. I told her about your interest in working there and she said they always need therapists to work with children and teens. Here's Bill's phone number if you want to call him for more information."

I nearly fainted and was speechless, which rarely happens to me. After the shock wore off and I was able to formulate a coherent sentence I said, "Wow that's great news, but what brought about the change of heart in you? You have always made it perfectly clear that you thought a career change was a bad idea." Patrick's response was not as deep as I thought it might have been and he replied, "I am tired of you being weird and sad about your work."

I wasted no time, just in case Patrick changed his mind, and called Bill that night. I had difficulties understanding Bill on the phone that night. I later found out about his diagnosis of a muscle deterioration disease which affected his voice. Bill was so helpful in giving me information about the clinic. I told him I had been on the clinic website but was unable to find out how to apply for a position. He told me, "Oh, we hire by word of mouth. I can pitch your resume at our next staff meeting. Do you have your resume?" I was so thankful that I had updated my resume last week and told him, "Yes I do."

Patrick passed my resume along to Amy and Amy passed it on to Bill and about 10 days later I received a call from the office manager to arrange an interview! I learned that when I let go and let God be in charge things happen fast. Letting go reminds me of the country song about Jesus taking the steering wheel of the car from the distressed driver. To me it means getting out of the driver's seat of life and sitting in the passenger seat or even sitting in the back seat while Jesus is in total control of the steering, gas and brake pedal. If I just took my hands off the steering wheel of my life it would be too easy to grab it back and do things my way. This is something that I work on a great deal. God's ways, God's timing, and God's love is perfect. *"I will instruct you and teach you in the ways you should go: I will counsel you and watch over you." Psalm 32:8*

I was hired at the clinic in April and tried to negotiate a deal with the school I was working at to do part-time counseling at both places. Initially, I was given a green light to pursue both positions from the school superintendent. However, in June the part time school counseling offer was rescinded and my first-grade teaching position was the only job opportunity at the school.

What to do? Forget my dream job because I felt like I needed the financial security of keeping my school job? I shed a few tears and then sought some Godly counseling from a couple who I adopted as my parents. *"Plans fail for lack of counsel, but with many advisors they succeed." Proverbs 15:22.* Their names are Cliff and Ferne and they really didn't need another daughter because they already had three grown daughters, grandchildren and great grandchildren. However, they accepted the position as adopted parents and we are very close.

At the time we lived in the same subdivision and I walked over and shared my dilemma. They were perfectly clear in telling me they would not tell me what to do. That was something I had to figure out myself. As I was blubbering through my story, I mentioned that I kept getting this vision from a past sermon at church. It went something like this: there is a fable of a monkey who tried to get a few grapes out of a thin necked jar to eat. He could get his hand in, but when he tried to get his hand out with a fist full of grapes his hand got stuck and he was unable to get the grapes out of the jar. The message I received was I was like the monkey holding on a few mushy rotten grapes which represented my work at school, while a beautiful vista of rolling hills and acres and acres of grapevines loaded with beautiful ripe grapes beckoned me to move over there. These grapevines represented the new work at the clinic. When I shared this part, Cliff said, "Wait! Stop! What did you just say?"

I repeated the vision and he said that is a message from God. Grapes in the Bible represent Godly works of the Israelites in the Old Testament. Could God, the Creator of heaven and earth be guiding and leading me in the direction He wanted me to go? Was my work at the school completely finished? Is this an answer to the prayer for fresh work and expanding my territory? My mind and heart were reeling with questions and possibilities.

I had the gift of time to make a final decision because it was summer break. I told the school superintendent that I would let him know at the end of the summer what my decision was. Since I was hired at the clinic I began working there on July 7. As I prepared for this new adventure, I poured on the prayer. I saw the counseling opportunity as a partnership with God. God was the brains and heart of the operation and I was to be the hands and feet. I prayed for His wisdom, His heart, His Strength and Courage. I prayed for ways to repurpose my school resources to work in my counseling office. I prayed for a smooth transition from public education to a medical clinic. I prayed for a tangible confirmation that I was supposed to resign from the school. I spent extended time in my morning devotion, anywhere from an hour to three hours. I prayed about each patient and how best to help each one and each day at the clinic I became more comfortable.

After about three weeks of work at the clinic, one of the office staff said to me, "Jill, have you looked at your schedule recently?" My schedule of patients was on the computer and I was looking at it. "Yes, a little bit." I responded. "Well, I just want you to know that your schedule is full, like someone who has been here for five years," she said.

With a big smile and a grateful heart, I said," That's great! God wants me to be here!"

She said, "Not only does He want you here, but so do we. You have been the best new therapist we have ever had." God is so faithful! That was my tangible confirmation to retire from teaching.

I retired from public education the summer of 2014 and worked, in partnership, with God at the clinic for three years. Every time I walked into the clinic to work, I would invite the Holy Spirit to join each session. This one act allowed a sense of peace and calm to be present each work day in my office. Great spiritual growth transpired as I sought God's heart, not my own heart to help my clients. I came to lovingly refer to my clients as my peeps.

God helped me see through His eyes on many occasions. Like how many of our wrong decisions come from listening to the lies of Satan. He is the father of lies. Many of my teen peeps believed the lies that all teens must be sexually active to fit in and the goal in high school was to be popular. I loved encouraging them to be the best version of themselves and to tell them how God had created them *fearfully and wonderfully Psalm 139:14* with a unique set of qualities. God says, *"For I know the plans I have for you, plans to prosper you and not to harm you, plans to give you a hope and a future."* *Jeremiah 29:11.*

Another revelation from God during that time was that each one of us carries around a wounded heart. Past experiences have affected us, sometimes in positive ways and sometimes in negative ways. The negative experiences have left emotional scars which affect our actions today. Christ wants us to be set free from our past sin, from shame and live with no condemnation. In Romans 8 it states, *"Therefore there is no condemnation for those who are in Christ Jesus, because through Christ Jesus the law of the Spirit of life set me free from the law of sin and death."* I have come to realize people are at all different levels of spiritual and moral development and it shows in their actions and words. I can have compassion and pray for people who are stuck in negativity.

PARTNERSHIP WITH GOD

What does the word partnership mean? Here is the dictionary definition: the state of being a partner and the definition of a partner is a person who takes part in an undertaking with another or others, especially in a business or company with the shared risk of profit or loss. Why would God, who is all powerful even want or need to partner with his creation? It is for a believer's growth and maturity. God intentionally equips each person with a unique personality and talents to do the work he had preplanned for us. *"continue to work out your salvation with fear and trembling, for it is God who works in you to will and to act according to his good purpose."* *Philippians 2:12-13*

God, who is all powerful, chooses to partnership with us to accomplish His will. There are so many examples of this in the Bible. God worked through Moses to set the Israelites free from Egypt. God could have just eliminated the king of Egypt, but He didn't. Moses was apprehensive about the assignment God had given him and believed he was ill equipped for the task. However, God empowered

Moses to lead the people out of slavery and become their Godly leader in the desert.

Another example of partnership from the Old Testament is from the book of Nehemiah. God gave Nehemiah the burden to repair the demolished wall around Jerusalem after the exiles had returned from captivity from Babylon. Nehemiah left an important job in the Persian government and in just 52 days organized, managed, supervised, encouraged, met opposition, and confronted injustice to completely rebuild the wall. Nehemiah was a person God could depend on in the world.

God asks us, His children, to be determined to accept His invitation to partner with Him to help spread the Good News of Jesus Christ and live a life intimately connected to Him. To be determined means making the decision to do something and then doing the hard work to achieve that decision. I decided to trust Jesus as my Lord and Savior. The hard work is seeking Him daily by reading the Bible and other writings about Him, obeying the word, praying, journaling, pondering His ways, going to church, and teaching His word. I have found the hard work is the way I live my life. It is not a burden, it brings me peace and security. *"And the peace of God, which transcends all understanding, will guard your hearts and your minds in Christ Jesus." Philippians 4:7*

In the new testament, God chose Mary, the mother of Jesus, to partner with Him and the Holy Spirit to give birth to the Son of God! Luke tells us in chapter one how Mary was visited by the Angel Gabriel. Gabriel tells Mary she is highly favored, and the Lord was with her. She would give birth to a son and to give him the name Jesus. Jesus would be called the Son of the Most High and his reign over his kingdom will never end.

Mary was confused at this announcement because she was a virgin, young and poor, all qualities that made her an unlikely candidate for God's service. The angel Gabriel explained how *"the Holy Spirit would come upon her and the power of the Most High would overshadow her and the holy one born to her would be called the Son of God." Luke 1:35. "For nothing is impossible <u>with</u> God." Luke 1:37*

Mary's responded, *"I am the Lord's servant. May it be to me as you have said." Luke 1:38*

Mary's act of obedience required faith and trust. A young unmarried girl who became pregnant in her time would be rejected by her family, forced into begging or prostitution, or possibly stoned to death. She chose to step out in faith even if the outcome could be disastrous. Being highly favored by God doesn't mean an easy life, it means that God is with us, to guide us, to lead us, and help us to do impossible tasks sometimes. I hope, dear one, you will walk in obedience and accept the assignments prepared for you, as you partner with the God of the universe to do His will. *"I run in the path of your commands for you have set my heart free." Psalm 119:33*

SCRIPTURE ON STEWARDSHIP

I was plagued with money and financial worries for most of my adult life. It started, as I mentioned earlier, when my dad was ill and unable to work fulltime. I was in my late teen years. My fears grew when I went away to college and saw how other college kids were able to call home when they needed more money. That wasn't an option for me. I didn't mind working my way through college, however not having a financial safety net was stressful. I acquired my first credit card in college and to make ends meet I had some credit card debt when I graduated. When I married Patrick, I brought my financial insecurities with me. Since he was not harboring financial fears he spent money more freely than I did. This led to separate checking accounts, so I could be in control of the money I earned. We had this arrangement for many years, right up until we were saved in 2002. We then learned how God has a great deal to say about money.

Through sermons at church and a Christian financial class we have turned our views of finances from a worldly perspective to God's kingdom perspective. First and most importantly all we have, money, possessions, talents, and time are gifts from God. Right at the beginning of the Bible it says, *In the beginning God created the heavens and the earth. Genesis 1:1.* God has the absolute right and ownership over all He has created. God asks us, who are created in His image, to be stewards or managers of our possessions, the earth, and life itself. This is a mighty calling to join God in His purpose to redeem all the peoples of the earth.

Patrick and I now have a joint checking account in which we tithe regularly to our church and missionaries to further God's kingdom. We have adopted the lifestyle of "Less is Best" and have downsized our housing and possessions. We are a work in progress trying to live a simple life.

BODY OF CHRIST

"Just as each of us has one body with many members, and these members do not all have the same function, so in Christ we who are many form one body, and each member belongs to all the others." Romans 12:4-5.

Believers function as the body of Christ here on earth. Jesus resides up in heaven and in our hearts. Jesus depends on us, his followers, to be led by the Holy Spirit and be his hands and feet here on earth. The important thing to remember is each one of us is unique and has been anointed with different talents, interests, and giftings. It is our individual work, with the help of the Holy Spirit, to discover our gifts and to use them to further God's kingdom.

I have taken a gifts inventory and it pointed out teaching and encouraging as my strong points. I had already been a teacher for 15 years and had an encouraging way with my students before being saved, but now I had to learn how these gifts could be used in God's Kingdom. When I first was born again I was afraid to teach because of the verse in the Book of James, *"Not many of you should presume to be teachers, my brothers, because you know that we who teach will be judged more strictly."* James 3:1.

Honestly, I wasn't equipped to teach God's Word at that time. Now, I consider it an honor and privilege to teach the Word of God. It is a great responsibility to affect other's spiritual lives.

Partnering with other believers in the body of Christ is a way of life for Patrick and me. The fellowship and friends we have made in all the churches we have attended have had such a positive impact on our lives. God made us to be social beings, to share the good times and the hard times with others to receive and to give support and encouragement. *"And let us consider how we may spur one another on toward love and good deeds. Let us not give up meeting together as some are in the habit of doing but let us encourage one another—and all the more as you see the Day approaching." Hebrews 10:24-25*

THE BEST RELATIONSHIP

I have come to believe that my personal relationship with Jesus is the most important relationship in my life. God doesn't want us to just know about Him, He wants us to know Him in a personal relationship. Just like all great relationships, a personal relationship with Jesus is an "all in" type of thing. It's like running and jumping in a swimming pool; exciting, a little apprehension, and refreshing. Also, there's commitment, trust, communication, quality time, grace, mercy, and wonder.

My personal relationship with Christ began like most relationships with a curiosity and an attraction. Remember the happy and singing members at Hunter's Creek Church? I yearned for the joy they demonstrated with their words and actions. God already knew me, but I had to get to know Him. I got to know Him by reading His word, the Bible, learning to pray, spending time meditating on God, and feeling connected to Him while being out in nature. I slowly began to trust God with parts of my life. I remember having a "conversation" with Jesus and asking how much of Him needs to be in me. I was making guesses like 80% Jesus and 20% me or is it 90% Jesus and 10% me and then I felt the Holy Spirit convey to me that God is not about numbers. He wants all of me, so we can do beautiful work together. Beautiful work that resembles the amazing sunsets God creates at the end of each day. That excites me so much. How can the God of the universe want to do beautiful work with an ordinary woman like me?

The unconditional love of God is the best part of our relationship. God loves me, and you, when we are good, bad and everything in between. He never kicks us to the curb because of our mistakes and sin instead He lovingly picks us up, dries our tears, and gives us another opportunity to get it done His way, the right way. No person is capable of this kind of love it's God's perfect love. *"God is love. Whoever lives in love lives in God, and God in him."* 1 John 4:1

TROUBLES

Jesus promises believers, "*...in Me you may have peace. In this world you will have trouble. But take heart! I have overcome the world.*" *John 16:33.* Trusting Jesus as my Lord and Savior guarantees that He will never abandon me in times of struggle or trouble. I had to grow in this belief because when I was first saved, I was programmed to use my own will power and strength to accomplish all the tasks in my life, I needed reprogramming.

I recall being at a Wednesday night service focusing on heathy living and a question was presented to us, "What do you do first when beginning a healthy eating habit?" My mind went to a checklist: research about healthy eating plans, buy healthy foods, prepare healthy meals, use will power, etc. A mature Godly woman raised her hand to answer the question and her response was, "I pray."

"Wow," I thought, "I want to be like that. I want to go to God first with all matters in my life."

That was the seed of faith and trust planted in my heart and it was watered by sermons, other believers, and troubles in my life. My Bible notes say, troubles can be helpful. Troubles have a way of humbling me, helping me seek God's view, amping up my prayers, becoming more dependent on God and submitting to His purposes in my life.

Going through troubles and trials help us become more compassionate to others in trouble. This is by God's design as it is said in His word, *"Praise be to the God and Father of our Lord Jesus Christ, the Father of compassion and the God of all comfort, who comforts us in all our troubles, so that we can comfort those in any trouble with the comfort we ourselves have received from God."* 2 Corinthians 1:3-4.

God has used my past experience as an elementary school teacher and counselor to help mentor a bright and talented young teacher. This is a total God experience! I met this teacher at a church service. A little later I saw her at the knitting group (we both are knitting challenged) and talked some. Then while our church was serving meals to people without power during Hurricane Irma, she told me about her new job as a first-grade teacher after the original teacher went on a sick leave. I said, "I always thought it would be fun to be a classroom volunteer." She said, "Would you like to be my classroom volunteer?"

I thought about it for a nanosecond and said, "Sure."

God did a work in her, in me, and the students in her class. Words like, perseverance and patient endurance, encouragement, confidence in Christ, and prayer have been given to us through the Holy Spirit. We had become good friends who trusted in God's leading, wisdom and strength to teach and guide her students to have good character and master the grade level curriculum. When I walked up the sidewalk to the school entrance I'd say, "I am and Ambassador of Christ! Let my light shine brightly!"

IDOLS

God has a great deal to say about idols in the Bible. In Exodus 20 God spoke the words of The Ten Commandments. Verses 2-5 tell how God wants us to know He is the one and only true God.

"I am the Lord your God, who brought you out of Egypt, out of the land of slavery. You shall have no other gods before me. You shall not make for yourself <u>an idol</u> in the form of anything in heaven above or on earth beneath or in the waters below. You shall not bow down to them or worship them: for I the Lord your God, am a jealous God."

When the ten commandments were written God's people were worshiping many gods and they would build or make an idol to represent that god. For example, statues or poles made of metals, wood or stone would be worshiped. People would wear amulets, which are jewelry worn to ward off evil. Some people today still wear and believe in the power of amulets. However, God has stated His commandment to worship only Him.

Today people create idols when something or someone is taking up most of their time and energy. Things like money, fame, career, possessions or pleasure can be used for personal identity, be the meaning of life, or provide security and pride in a person's life. God wants us to make Him our central focus.

When Patrick and I built our "big" house on twelve acres in Michigan we originally thought we were building the American Dream: home ownership. We told family members and friends about our plans to create a golf course lawn from the cornfield we had bought. Most of them were skeptical, but we were determined to make it happen. We were not saved at this time, salvation came three years after purchasing the property and building our home.

We invested so much money, time, and sweat equity in our American dream. People we knew would give us compliments on the lawn and landscaping and it all went to our heads. We would do more improvements; finish the basement (with a second kitchen and bathroom), pave the driveway, install a sprinkler system, have a rail fence built, and the list goes on and on.

About eight years later and much learning about God's way of doing life, We realized the house and golf course lawn had become an idol. Patrick and I were sitting on the porch one fall day, admiring the yard, when I saw something on the grass. I stood up and pointed it out to Patrick. We rushed to the spot in the yard to find out the blemish in the yard was only an orange fall leaf that had blown in from the neighbor's tree.

"Oh my," I thought, "Our house has become too big of a thing in our lives." You see it had taken up so much of our time and energy and had become part of our identity. It had to go.

It was bittersweet when we sold it, but so necessary for us to live the God centered life written about in the Bible. We are not perfect but strive to live a simple life serving our Lord and Savior Jesus and others. We talk about how potential major purchases will impact the Kingdom of God and try to prevent any future idol worship.

FREEDOM

In many places in the Bible the concept of freedom is mentioned, such as:

"Now the Lord is the Spirit, and where the Spirit of the Lord is, there is freedom." 2 Corinthians 3:7

...Jesus said, "If you hold to my teaching, you are really my disciples. Then you will know the truth and the truth will set you free." John 8:31-32

I so want to help clear up any misconceptions you may have about freedom. Some people believe freedom is when a person can do whatever they want, whenever they want, wherever they want, as many times as they want and have a completely boundary free life where no one tells them what to do. In theory this sounds great, but scripturally, it is not freedom, but being chained to the consequences of sin. Let me illustrate this using a hot topic: sex.

Sex was created by God to be shared between a man and a woman who are married to show intimacy, love and create new life. Compare that to the complications and negative effects of sex outside these parameter; An unwanted pregnancy, emotional trauma and woundedness, false intimacy, venereal disease, sex addictions, pornography use, secrecy, and the list goes on. Can anyone, honestly, say that these just noted consequences are examples of freedom? No.

When a person trusts Jesus as their Lord and Savior and learns his teachings, and follows His ways of living, they are free! Free from the guilt and shame of poor decisions, free from regretful words and actions, free to seek the truth and respond accordingly. In Psalm 1 a blessed person is one who delights in the law of the Lord.

Dear one there are only two paths in life: God's path of obedience which leads to eternal life or a path of rebellion and destruction that leads to eternal death. That's it. There is no middle ground with God. Just as my search led me to this crossroads, you too must choose. I hope and pray that you choose a life built on the solid rock of Jesus. Or if you have already chosen Jesus as your Savior that you will want to keep going higher and deeper with Christ.

BE A BEREAN

What is a Berean? In Acts 17:10-11 Bereans are described as people of noble character. They also received the Good News of Jesus Christ with eagerness and examined the scriptures every day to see if what Apostle Paul was preaching to them was true. We hear so much information about God and Jesus and it can be confusing. It is our job, with the help of the Holy Spirit, to compare any and all spiritual information to what is written in the Bible. A message heard from a sermon, in a book, or even a fellow believer must not contradict what is written in the Bible. God's word is true and final.

While watching the sunset at the beach with some other believers, some information was shared. This information was about Noah's ark. One person claimed he had information that led him to believe there were no children at the time of the flood. I thought, "I never read that in the Bible." But kept listening.

The man continued to explain how he came up with this conclusion. It seemed maybe plausible, however, I went to the scriptures and commentaries about Noah's ark and none of the sources claimed there were no children at the time of the flood. We all hear claims of truth about God, be a Berean and check it out to make sure it is God's truth.

WORD OF THE YEAR

It was the Christmas season of 2016. I had read somewhere that a good tool for spiritual growth was to pick a word to focus on for an entire year. Since the new year of 2017 was approaching I thought I would try it out. Very quickly the word strength came to me. Both Patrick and I would need strength to close our counseling practices, pack up our household goods, rent a U-Haul, and drive to our new place in Florida. Patrick would also need extra strength for the 3-month remodeling phase.

It's amazing how The Holy Spirit worked at maturing me through this past year with a single word, strength. At first, I defined strength in the physical realm not the spiritual realm. I thought of packing and moving boxes from our 2nd story apartment, saying good bye to peeps, friends, and family, and Patrick being in Florida while I was still in Michigan. We did need strength for these activities, but not our finite strength that runs out like an empty tank of gas in a car. Or, human strength that gets discouraged. We needed the infinite power of God Almighty. In God's word many scriptures point out the truth about strength. Here are some that I had wrote in my 2017 journal.

> January 2 – *"Look to the LORD and HIS strength; seek His face always." Psalm 105:4*

> January 6 – *"Even youths grow tired and weary, and young men stumble and fall, But those who hope (wait) in the LORD will renew their strength." Isaiah 40:30*

> January 6 – *"Now to Jesus who is able to do immeasurably more than all we ask or imagine, according to His power that is at work within us…" Ephesians 3:20*

> January 7 – *"…O my Strength, come quickly to help me." Psalm 22:19*

> January 8 – *"God is our refuge and strength, an ever-present help in trouble." Psalm 46:1*

Do you see how quickly God corrected my faulty perspective of strength? Within the first 8 days of the new year I pressed into these promises and placed my faith firmly in God and His strength and vitality.

We would quickly need to be strong in the Lord emotionally. During the winter, between our two families, we had 5 funerals for elderly aunts and uncles and Patrick's dad. Most of the funerals did not come as surprises due to age and deteriorating health of these aunts and uncles. However, Harrold, my father-in-law had been doing well, considering he had many ailments, but he had declined quickly after his older brother, our Uncle Ed, died in January. Harrold died on March 6, 2017.

When older people die it can be a blessing and funerals can be a good experience. I never thought I would be writing that. I came to this observation by attending funerals with my mom. She liked to attend the funerals of her friends and acquaintances, but she didn't want to go alone. My two older sisters, Jenifer and Janet always found an excuse not to go and would say, "Ask Jill to go with you."

I would get asked and most of the time I did take my mom to these visitations and funerals. My mom enjoyed catching up with people she knew who had attended the funeral. On the drive home I would ask my mom, "What did you like about that funeral?" Then we would discuss what we both liked about the funeral. Years later at my mom's visitation and funeral, all the things she liked about funerals were included; her life in video pictures, lots of reminiscing, only one day for visitation, and a luncheon.

Back to 2017, Patrick grieved a little, survived the remodel, flew back to Michigan, and we finished packing. God gave us strength for all this and the actual drive to Florida with a U-Haul. Everything seemed to be moving smoothly. We unpacked and were feeling settled. We were making friends at church and in our neighborhood. I was trying out the local grocery stores and even found a Mennonite farm market close by.

IN GOD WE TRUST

Five weeks in our new Florida home then...Hurricane Irma was projected to hit our new home state of Florida as a category five hurricane. A hurricane with the wind speeds over 180mph. Many people from church initially thought they would ride out the storm but later evacuated. Patrick and I both felt led to eventually evacuate, too.

Early Wednesday, September 6, as we evacuated, my prayers to God went like this, "Lord, this is your house. If you want to blow it away I will have to accept that. Just know I will be very sad for a while and won't be able to help others. I pray that our villa looks just like it does know when we return." I made sure all the lights were turned off, looked the doors and we left at 3:00 am to miss the traffic leaving Florida. *"God is our refuge and strength. An ever-present help in trouble." Psalm 46:1*

This was our first experience with a hurricane and it was an eye-opening experience. First, it was a very long anxious wait for Irma to hit the United States. My neighbor, who had hurricane experience, helped us get prepared because we thought we were going to stay and ride the storm out. It was Friday, September 1 when these preparations began. I started loading gallon zip lock bags with ice from the icemaker in the freezer, putting candles in the kitchen, checking that we had matches and lighters, taking pictures of each room, just in case we had an insurance claim, and watching the weather channel. Watching the weather channel really set me on edge. I personally feel that the media overdramatizes what they report or that it is more opinion than facts. The more I watched and listened the more I became anxious and I finally had to limit my exposure to just the new updates and watch the weather models just once a day.

On our road trip back to Michigan to stay with my mother-in-law, I had a melt-down. Not a loud screaming one, just a whimpering, doubting cry in the car. Patrick looked over and said something so important, "I see your upset, but you're the girl who spends hours each morning with Jesus, reading, praying, and journaling. Don't you think you need to draw on God's strength and have faith that this will all work out?" I sat up straighter and thought, "He's right! I KNOW JESUS! And it made all the difference! I can remain active, joyous, and content in all circumstances. I'm acting like this is a hopeless situation, but I serve The God of all Hope. I run on faith." Right then I started praying and asking God to impart more of His protection and wisdom to help me grow in faith and trust during this time.

Patrick and I also took an on-line Christian based crisis response training offered free to people at our church during this time. This training taught me so much about natural disasters and how unsaved people are more open to seeking God and trusting Jesus as their Savior at times of crisis. I also learned the first action step this crisis organization takes is to pray to mitigate or lessen the disaster. I truly believe the combined prayers from believers all over the world lessened the effects of Hurricane Irma. Persistent and boldness in prayer can change circumstances.

All weather reports predicted catastrophic devastation to the entire state and while there was major damage in some areas it was substantially less in others, to the amazement of the meteorologists. I remember watching a news cast and when the meteorologist was asked his opinion about the lessened effects of Hurricane Irma he was practically speechless and shrugged his shoulders basically saying that science had no answers. The miracles of God usually do leave people in awe.

I drew comfort and strength from some specific verses in the Bible while waiting out the storm back in Michigan;

"Which of you fathers, if your son asks for a fish, will give him a snake instead? Or if he asks for an egg, will give him a scorpion? If then, though you are evil, know how to give good gifts to your children, how much more will your Father in heaven give the Holy Spirit to those who ask Him?" Luke 11:11 I have a good, good Heavenly Father who loves me.

"The LORD is a refuge for the opposed, a stronghold in times of trouble. Those who know Your Name will trust in You, for You, LORD have never forsaken those who seek You." Psalm 9:9-10 I may have loss or suffering, but God is with me always.

Here's part of my journal entry for Sunday, September 10, 2017, the day Hurricane Irma hit Florida.

Dear Lord,

I love you! I trust you! Before I watch the news to see what Hurricane Irma has done, I trust that you have good plans for us, hope and a future planned with Your good works. Whatever has happened, I KNOW You will be with us. You work all things for good to us who love you. You are a good good Father.

Here are some things I have learned from this crisis:

YOU are in control
In YOU I have peace
Storms build faith muscles
I used to run from danger
The media hypes me up
Stuff is stuff and it all belongs to YOU
Keep close to YOU for I am weak
This is the year of YOUR STRENGTH
Don't be financially strapped
People are important
Venice is our home
We run on Faith!
Be persistent in prayer
       Love,
       Jilly

Praise GOD! Our community was hit by a category 2 hurricane, not the category 5 that was predicted. Our villa received no damage and never lost power. We were fired up to return to Florida. We helped others in our community who were without power, with our church family, by serving meals and praying with others. God takes us through challenging situations so that we can be empathetic and have compassion for others. Again, the verse in 2 Corinthians came to my mind, *"Praise be to the God and Father of our Lord Jesus Christ, the Father of compassion and the God of all comfort, who comforts us in all our troubles, so that we can comfort those in any trouble with the comfort we ourselves have received from God."* God's comfort can be the taking away of our troubles but more often it's receiving strength, encouragement, and hope to deal with our troubles.

For the year 2018 I have chosen the word wonder to focus on and Patrick found my theme song.

I Wonder as I Wander under the Sky
How Jesus, the Savior did come for to die
For poor ordinary people like you and like I
I Wonder as I wander out under the sky.

LIVE FREE

I was using my exercise ball one day and noticed the *go fit* label on it. It got me thinking about adding one more letter and making it GOD FIT. That led to more thinking and pondering of what would it mean to be GOD FIT? Two scriptures came to my mind.

Jesus replied, "Love the Lord your God with all your heart and with all your soul and with all your mind. This is the first and greatest commandment. And the second is like it: Love your neighbor as yourself." Matthew 22:37-39.

"The most important commandment," answered Jesus, "Is this, O Israel, the Lord our God, the Lord is one. Love the Lord your God with all your heart and with all your soul and with all your mind and with all your strength." Mark 12:29-30

In my mind being GOD FIT means having my entire being; mind, body, soul, spirit, strength, talents, and time focused on God then I am ready and able to hear, accept and complete the assignments He has planned for me. I became GOD FIT and stay GOD FIT by completing my daily to do list: bible reading/study, journaling or writing, some type of physical workout (30-60 minutes) preferably outside, healthy eating, rated G media and reading, and putting God and people first. Dear Ones, God has plans and a purpose for your life, too. I hope and pray that you will commit to being GOD FIT for life.

WAIT

Waiting is not something most of us like to do, myself included. However, God has enlightened me on the benefits of waiting. I had to get the Godly perspective on waiting not the worldly perspective. Before Christ in my life I viewed waiting as sitting around twiddling my thumbs, watching the clock, or pacing the floor. Others honk their car horns, huff and puff, or even get pushy. All of these are basically negative and nonproductive activities. Then I heard a sermon at church about waiting. Waiting is wonderful because it's active not passive. The Pastor used the illustration of a waiter or waitress in a restaurant who is active serving others by taking orders, delivering food, clearing tables, and calculating the tab. There is no sitting around on a waiter or waitresses shift at a restaurant because if the restaurant is slow they even set tables, wipe menus, or clean, there's always something to do.

So, when we are tested by God's perfect timing and find ourselves waiting we should be active serving others, reading our Bibles, praying, learning, staying put, patiently anticipating, or even pondering the purpose of the waiting. The Bible has many verses about waiting:

"I _waited_ patiently for the LORD:
He turned to me and heard my cry." Psalm 40:1

"I _wait_ for the LORD, my soul _waits,_
And in His word I put hope." Psalm 130:5

"...while we _wait_ for the blessed hope-the glorious appearing of our great God and Savior, Jesus Christ..." Titus 2:13

After Patrick and I had sold our Michigan house that we had built we rented an apartment. We didn't have a clear direction at that time in our life. My mom had died, I tried to run back to Arizona by interviewing for a job out there (I didn't get it, Praise God), and I was tired of the maintenance and upkeep on a house with a large yard.

We had a walking route from the apartment we rented, and it crossed two main streets with crosswalks. These crosswalks had the visual walk and don't walk signs and an audible mechanical voice that said, "WAIT"..."WAIT"..."WAIT" when it was not our turn to walk. We interpreted the "WAIT" as a message from God. He was asking us to take some time before we made our next move. I am so thankful we waited because we eventually found a condo, in Michigan, that fit our needs and led us to our next season living closer to Patrick's parents.

I like to use God's creation to help remember His ways of living. The turtle is a slow but determined animal and I came up with this poetry to help me slow down and wait.

<u>S</u>urrender and submit to God

Look up and listen to God

Obey God

Wait on God's perfect timing

Another waiting example I have from my personal life is from past experiences of walking my dog Gretta. I learned, while attending puppy school with her, dogs are supposed to walk beside their master. We were instructed and practiced training our puppies to do just that, no running ahead and pulling on the leash and no lagging behind. Gretta obeyed most of the time except when we got close to home and she would be set free in the yard. Then she would pull and strain on her collar and I would jerk the leash trying to get her to comply and walk next to me.

Gretta was a German Shepherd and very strong and strong-willed. It was so irritating for me and then I felt God remind me that is how He feels when I run ahead of Him or lag behind HIM. I felt so convicted to make my best effort to walk in *God's Highway of Holiness* hand in hand with HIM. I am far from perfect from achieving this goal, but I know the wonderful peace and joy of obeying God and His perfect timing.

WHITE FUNERAL

Jesus says to us, *"If anyone would come after me, he must deny himself and take up his cross daily and follow me. For whoever wants to save his life will lose it, but whoever loses his life for me will save it." Luke 9:23-24.* By choosing to become a disciple of Jesus Christ each of us puts aside our selfish desires and replaces them with serving God and His purpose. This is a daily process which requires us to nail our bad habits and any sin that hinders our service to God to the cross of Christ. Remember Jesus died on the cross for our sins.

I have a journal entry that I titled, "My White Funeral." In it, I wrote a letter to God claiming the death of my "self" or "flesh."

Dear Lord,

I lay my "self" at the foot of your cross. It's dead! Finally, Lord have Your Way in me! I rebuke, "self" and Satan. I am totally Yours. Rush in like a mighty power to do life Your Way! I am free to be the best version You have for me! I worship You JESUS MY LORD, MY SAVIOR, MY TEACHER, AND MY FRIEND FOREVER AND EVER!

I drew a grave stone with these words on it, "Jill's Pride and Prejudice Dead on Arrival." As I encounter challenges and troubles in life I try to remember how God loves everyone and I ask in prayer how God wants me to respond. To me, following Christ is an exciting way to live. *"For to me, to live is Christ and to die is gain." Philippians 1:21*

SPIRITUAL WARFARE

As my faith in God has reached higher and grown deeper and I have become bolder for Jesus, a certain someone is not happy. This certain someone is Satan. He is called the Father of Lies, the devil, and has followers called demons. He is the head fallen angel who tried to become an equal to God. He is the enemy of God and all the people who claim faith in Jesus Christ.

When I was enduring my long refinement, I trusted the scripture in *Ephesians 6*. Apostle Paul writes, *"Finally, be strong in the Lord and in His mighty power. Put on the full armor of God so that you can take your stand against the devil's schemes." V. 10-11.* I drew an illustration of myself wearing the armor of God: the belt of truth, the breastplate of righteousness, the sword of the Spirit, sandals of the gospel of peace, helmet of salvation, and the shield of faith. I kept this drawing in my desk for a ready reminder to stand firm against the devil's schemes.

These schemes come in the form of fear, panic, discouragement, mental confusion, roller coaster feelings, and indecisiveness, all of which destroy faith and paralyze the believer. God's word gives the believer power to combat spiritual warfare:

"Submit yourselves then to God. Resist the devil and he will flee from you." James 4:7

"Is any one of you in trouble? He should pray." James 5:13

"So do not fear, for I am with you; Do not be dismayed, for I am your God. I will strengthen you and help you; I will uphold you with my righteous right hand." Isaiah 41:10

"God is love. Whoever lives in love lives in God, and God in him." 1 John 4:16

Each believer needs to suit up daily, pray, sing songs of praise, and walk this life out in the power of God's love. Remember this: anyone committed to God should expect Satan's attacks.

"Perfect love drives out fear," 1 John 4:18

"Finally, brothers whatever is true, whatever is noble, whatever is right, whatever is pure, whatever is lovely, whatever is admirable-if anything is excellent or praiseworthy-think about such things." Philippians 4:8

EVANGELISM

Evangelism is defined as the preaching of the Lord with the intention of exposing God's love to all mankind through Jesus Christ. It's sharing the Good News that Jesus died on the cross to pay the penalty for all the sin of mankind, past, present and future. When I first got saved I was, what some people would call "on fire" for the Lord. I shared my new faith in Jesus Christ with some fellow teachers, the janitor, and friends. I wanted them to know the Good News. Some rejected the news, but my best friend accepted the gift and has been climbing the mountain, just like me.

I was very reluctant to share this Good News with my Catholic family, so I didn't for several months. Patrick and I started attending Hunter's Creek Community Church on Sundays and I avoided my family. It wasn't really working because I felt like I was sneaking around. Finally, my sister Jenifer called and asked about my church attendance and I had to be honest about our leaving the Catholic Church. This information was not well received to say the least.

My mom said, "Your father is rolling over in his grave at this news." My sister Janet called me a heretic. We were disowned by my family for several years. Patrick's family was a little more understanding since his sister and two of his brothers had changed Christian denominations. My family shunning us, pushed us closer to our new faith in Jesus and to our new Christian friends.

At the different churches I have attended each has preached sermons about evangelism. Some Christians are gifted in evangelism and it becomes their vocation or career. However, all other Christians are called and commanded to take part in personal evangelism, sharing the Good News of Jesus Christ with the unsaved people who are in our circle of life. My history with personal evangelism has vacillated between "on fire" and a pile of ashes and everything in between. I haven't been consistently concerned with peoples' eternity and that bothers me. In the spring of 2017, I was challenged to be more consistent by a sermon given by Mark Cahill.

I have heard Mark preach two times at New Life Christian Fellowship Church in Grand Blanc, Michigan. He is an evangelist with a heart for the lost of this world. The second time I heard him, he started his sermon by telling the congregation, "Today you will learn about the prayer of BOB." Our pastor's name was Bob, so I thought it was going to be about our Pastor's health, but I was wrong. The prayer of BOB was a way to become more evangelistic.

The first B stands for burden. Mark asked all who were listening to have a concern for people who did not know Jesus. He quoted this scripture, "*Whoever believes in the Son has eternal life, but whoever rejects the Son will not see life, for God's wrath remains on him.*" *John 3:36*. I thought, "I need to pray for this burden for the lost because some days it's not even on my radar screen." People I know, who do not accept Jesus as their Savior, will spend eternity in hell. When worded that way, I feel the burden.

The O in the prayer for BOB stands for opportunity. The opportunity to tell others about the Good News of Jesus Christ. In Colossians 4:2-4, Paul, the Apostle, writes, *"Devote yourselves to prayer, being watchful and thankful. And pray for us, too, that God may open a door for our message, so that we may proclaim the mystery of Christ, for which I am in chains. Pray that I may proclaim it clearly, as I should."* I have found opportunities to tell others about Jesus are everywhere, as I have grown closer in relationship to Jesus. Just like we talk about family and friends who are close to us, if we have a close and personal relationship with Jesus we can talk about Him.

The last B stands for BOLDNESS. Mark pointed out more of Apostle Paul's prayers, which are prayers for all believers, *"Pray also for me, that whenever I open my mouth, words may be given me so that I will fearlessly make known the mystery of the gospel, for which I am an ambassador in chains. Pray that I may declare it fearlessly, as I should." Ephesians 6:19-20.* Fearlessly was written twice to show believers the importance of being bold for Christ. *"...If God is for us who can be against us? Romans 8:31.* Satan is against all evangelistic work. The more people trust Jesus as their Lord and Savior, the more they turn away from sin and immorality.

As I listened to this sermon my heart was stirred, in a good way. Mark shared some powerful personal stories about talking to complete strangers about Jesus. I forgot to mention that Mark Cahill is also an author, who writes about salvation. As he concludes his message of salvation with strangers, he gives them one of his books to learn more about Jesus. "That's it. I need something to give to people when I share the mystery and wonder of Christ." I thought. I imagined a postcard or a bookmark, maybe there is something on-line that I can buy. Well…God had a bigger plan, a more meaningful and personal way to share my faith in Him. It's this book you are reading!

I pray that you are stirred up about the wonder and mystery of Jesus. I pray that you either choose to be born again and join the family of God for the first time *"I tell you the truth no one can see the kingdom of God unless he is born again." John 3:3* Or if you are already a son or daughter of God that you choose to climb higher on the mountain and dig deeper into your relationship with Jesus. I leave you with the final words of Jesus in the book of Matthew,

"All authority in heaven and on earth has been given to me. Therefore, go and make disciples of all nations, baptizing them in the name of the Father and the Son and of the Holy Spirit, and teaching them to obey everything I have commanded you. And surely I am with you always, to the very end of the age." Matthew 28:19-20

FROM GLORY TO GLORY

During a small group discussion, we were asked to share a Bible verse that came to our minds about enjoying the journey with Jesus. One woman shared the following verse:

Jesus tells us in the Bible, *"Enter through the narrow gate. For wide is the gate and broad is the road that leads to destruction, and many enter through it. But small is the gate and narrow the road that leads to life, and only a few find it." Matthew 7:13-14.*

Jesus is the gate. Believing in Jesus is the only way to get to heaven. He died on the cross for our sins and made us in right relationship with God. This may seem constricting, only one way to heaven, but it is not. When is anything in life a sure thing? People joke that only death and taxes are a sure thing, but I know different. Trusting Jesus as my Lord and Savior is a sure and real choice. The other members in the group that night shared how real and meaningful their lives were as they traveled on the narrow road.

The day after this small group meeting, I was pondering this verse as I was biking along a canal. To me, the water in the canal represented the narrow road. I began to think about my best decision to choose Jesus and travel His Highway of Holiness. Then I noticed a smooth path of water in the middle of the canal water. I looked at it and looked at it and finally stopped and took a picture of it. I sensed a Holy Spirit teaching moment coming, "within the narrow road is an even more narrow road for those who choose to go deeper and higher with Jesus."

"I choose this narrow road within the narrow road!" I answered back in my spirit.

I am physically living on earth but choose to be kingdom minded. I want to keep traveling the Highway of Holiness with Jesus. This glorious revelation from the Holy Spirit felt like a spiritual reward and I treasure it in my heart.

I'm ready to put closure to this book. I shared in the introduction how I moved to Florida with an open mind, heart, and schedule. Well, within a year's time God has filled my life and my husband's life with His purposes. We both volunteered at public schools and after school programs, we helped at a food pantry, with the landscaping team, and we have co-led small home groups with other believers. I joined the Wednesday night Bible teaching team and co taught in the preschool kid's church room. I assist with a Good News Bible Club at a local elementary school and entertain babies at a home for single moms. We have the opportunity to socialize every day of the week, if we wanted to. Our schedule is full of kingdom work and our reward is building treasure in heaven. I love living in a place that is forever summer with the sun and beach. A group of us meet Sunday evenings for sunset and socializing. My catch phrase is, "We live here!"

God is so good all the time! As Patrick and I press in and on with our relationship with Christ we feel a stirring of something new and great in the future. We wait for God's perfect timing. I hope by telling my story you will choose to become a part of HIS story. The best is yet to come.

"So whether you eat or drink or whatever you do, do it all for the glory of God." 1Corinthians 10:31

"So do not be ashamed to testify about our Lord." 2Timothy 1:8

ROMANS ROAD

For those of you who are ready for the adventure of living the abundant life with Christ I have included the Bible scriptures from the Book of Romans called the Romans Road. By reading, understanding and accepting these scriptures and praying to God about your need to be born again, you too can join the family of God.

Romans 3:23
For all have sinned and fall short of the glory of God.

Romans 6:23
For the wages of sin is death, but the gift of God is eternal life in Christ Jesus our Lord.

Romans 5:8
But God demonstrates his own love for us in this: While we were still sinners, Christ died for us.

Romans 10:9-10
If you declare with your mouth, "Jesus is Lord," and believe in your heart that God raised him from the dead, you will be saved. For it is with your heart that you believe and are justified.

Sample Prayer of Salvation

Lord,

I need you. I'm tired of trying to do my life in my own strength. I know I have sinned by thinking, saying, and doing things that displease you. Please forgive me of these sins I have committed against you. I believe Jesus Christ is your Son and He died on the cross for my sins and rose from the dead so that I can eternal life. I proclaim my faith in Jesus Christ for my salvation. Thank you for your love, mercy, and grace. I pledge to be forever faithful to Jesus my Lord and Savior. In the name of Jesus, I pray. Amen.

There! You are born again! The Holy Spirit now resides in you to be your inside guide. Please tell others what you have done, buy a Bible, shop around for a local Bible believing church to attend and to serve in, and be prepared to meet a whole bunch of new brothers and sisters! I pray you grow in relationship to the Extraordinary God. I hope you sign the salvation list and pass this book onto someone you know who needs Jesus!

I have accepted the Salvation provide by Jesus Christ

Name _____Date _____

Name _____Date _____

Name _____Date_____

Name _____Date_____

NOTES

Chapter 7 Refinement

Richard Blackaby, *Unlimiting God* (Colorado: Multnomah Books, 2008),
85-87.

Sarah Young, Jesus Calling (Tennessee: Thomas Nelson Books, 2004).

Chapter 25 Evangelism

Mark Cahill, Sermon for B.O.B.
(MarkCahill.org/teachings/sermons) May 2017.

Made in the USA
Monee, IL
18 November 2019

16918104R00092